THE VOICE OF SOUTHERN GOSPEL MUSIC

SINGING NEWS
presents

Praise

REPORTS

Inspiring REAL-LIFE STORIES
of How GOD ANSWERS *Prayer*

xulon
PRESS

To order additional copies,
please call 866-909-BOOK (2665).

Singing News is proud to present *Praise Reports*. This remarkable book compiles stories of how God performed miracles in the lives of ordinary individuals—people just like you.

Our editors trolled hundreds of submissions from people who wrote in to share a time when God touched their life, or the life of someone they know, supernaturally.

As you turn the pages of this book, we hope it blesses you beyond measure and encourages you to write down your own Praise Reports in the future!

—Singing News Editorial Team

Table of Contents

A Gift of Love

By Linda Andreas

My husband's health was deteriorating at a rapid rate. The resulting surgery and chemotherapy from his Hodgkin's cancer in 1990 had taken a toll on his body. Then diabetes was discovered, and this disease rapidly began to do its destruction within his body. A limited menu of foods, then pills, and finally insulin shots still resulted in his kidney failure.

Ron went on dialysis in September of 2003. This procedure, done four times a day at home, was very wearing on both of us. Ron had to retire from his plumbing/welding job with the union and stay close to home most of the time. However, we found a way to still do some traveling and enjoyed life as we took it—each day at a time.

We prayed for an answer and were led to investigate the possibility of a kidney transplant. We were told the wait would probably be at least five years. I made the decision to be tested as a match for my husband. After many tests, both psychological and physical, it was determined that indeed my kidney was a match for Ron. However, they were concerned about my previous breast cancer of nine years earlier. After prayer on our part, and discussion with many doctors, it was finally agreed upon by the medical profession that this kidney transplant could move forward. In the process of being tested, the doctors found a major problem with one of Ron's main arteries to his heart. He had double bypass heart surgery in February 2004 so he could survive the kidney transplant, which came in August 2004.

The transplant was a success! We are both doing well three years later and praise the Lord for His goodness to us. Although Ron still deals with various health issues, his quality of life has greatly improved.

We thank the Lord each day for the gift of life I was allowed to give to my husband.

Linda Andreas and her husband, Ron, live in Mason, Michigan, and have two married children, Troy and Tara, and an 18-month-old granddaughter, Alyssa. Andreas has been a legal secretary with the Attorney General's Office for thirty-four years. She is a member of the Eden United Brethren Church, where she is involved in choir and many other ministries.

Following Him

By Sharon Baker and Nan Rich

Our lives were forever changed in 1997! Although we had been friends for a number of years, this did not prepare us for what was about to happen. The Lord suddenly called Sharon's husband home, and within a year He took Nan's mom home. Our grief brought us closer together, but over the next two years we found ourselves on a downward spiral of emotional turmoil. In the midst of our most difficult days, the Lord challenged us with a vision to reach our community for Him. We found ourselves praying daily for direction as to how the Lord would use us in this way.

We had two strong common loves in our lives. First and foremost was our love for the Lord. Second was our love for southern gospel music. In prayer, we focused to see if God would open doors for us to reach our community through southern gospel. The Lord guided us every step of the way. We had no money, no experience, and not even the slightest knowledge of what it would take to become promoters, but the Lord had already determined to give us the privilege to host some of the biggest names in the ministry of southern gospel. We both felt very strongly the Lord would give us answers when we were led to the 2000 National Quartet Convention. Wow! Did we get an answer!

When we first entered the convention hall, Jason Waldroup of Greater Vision unexpectedly approached us and said a man had just come to their booth asking why Greater Vision didn't come to the Chicagoland area. You cannot imagine how we felt when Jason actually remembered us from a Greater Vision concert our church held well before that convention. That was all it took! We knew God had answered our prayer and given us direction. We knew He wanted to use us to bring in His ministers of the gospel through music and word.

Fishnet Promotions officially started in 2001. We are now in our seventh year and are continually amazed by God's hand in our efforts. Evidence of His provision was clear. Financial obligations were met at times in unexplainable ways, there were venues to hold our concerts, we had family and friends to help us, and there were Christian accountants and equipment for advertising. There were answers to our prayer at every turn! One key verse from Matthew 4:19 has kept us on track: "'Come, follow me,' Jesus said, 'And I will make you fishers of men.'"

We are two everyday ladies with outside jobs, families, and households to manage. We have frequent ups and downs. We've had individual trials, such as the death of our loved ones, major illnesses, and financial crises, but through it all, the Lord continues to bless us with the privilege of serving Him in this way. Time and time again He answers our prayers, even when our faith falls short and Satan works overtime to discourage us through various means.

Each concert shows us what the Lord will do when we are obedient to His calling. We see people come to a concert burdened down and leave with joy in their hearts. We are blessed by how much people are excited to have southern gospel concerts brought to them in an area where there is no other means to hear this wonderful music. Just knowing we are being used to uplift and strengthen His people to go and spread the Good News of Jesus Christ is a privilege. Our continued prayer is that our community will see their need for a Savior as we follow Him in this endeavor.

Sharon Baker has been widowed for ten years. She has one son and a new mother-in-law. Nan Rich has been married for thirty-nine years. She has two children and a granddaughter on the way. Both authors live in Wood Dale, Illinois.

Breaking Satan's Bondage

By Carolyn S. Belch

My 27-year-old son had been addicted to illegal drugs since the age of sixteen. Satan had him bound so tight that he could not reason everyday normal living skills. He repeatedly stole from his parents, sister, and anyone else he could hoodwink. This type of behavior eventually got him in trouble with the legal system. Even after pulling thirty days in jail nothing mattered to him except where was he going to get his next drug fix for a temporary high, irregardless of the consequences.

Praise God Almighty, He intervened in my son's life and gave him the wake-up call he needed one afternoon in October 2006. He awoke in the hospital after injecting heroine and cocaine the night before, but did not know where he was or how he got there. Later, I filled him in on the details. After I told him I had had to call the rescue squad to help resuscitate him because I couldn't rouse him, he had a wake-up call from heaven.

I want to sing the praises of Bethel Colony of Mercy in Lenoir, North Carolina, for providing the safe haven of a Christian transformation center. They enabled my son to obtain biblical knowledge that helps him walk safely with our Lord and Savior, Jesus Christ, daily.

Professionally, I work as a nurse, but on a weekly basis I travel the state singing gospel music and witnessing to people about Jesus and all He has done for my family. Through this singing adventure I have seen many lives touched with the healing of the Holy Spirit, and many lives saved with salvation for the body of our heavenly Father's kingdom.

Carolyn S. Belch lives in Greenville, North Carolina. She has worked at East Carolina University Brody School of Medicine in the endocrinology division as a staff nurse for eight years. She has been married to her husband Carl for thirty-one years. They have two grown children, Missy and Charles.

Four More Days

By Jessica Black

I'm a college student, and trying to figure out what to study and where to study is not as easy as it may seem. Right after high school I decided I was going to attend Liberty University in good ol' Virginia! My parents packed all of my stuff in their van, and we drove from the coast of North Carolina to the mountains of Virginia. I loved being in such a wonderful atmosphere, but after a while it started to get really expensive for my parents. They informed me they would no longer be able to pay for my tuition! I was crushed! I asked God to show me His will, but I didn't sit still and quiet enough for Him to answer my request. I started researching other schools and decided to move to Florida with my grandparents and attend the University of South Florida.

I visited the school and was prepared to transfer most of my credits, but something just didn't feel right. When I asked God to show me this time, I waited to see! Four days before I was supposed to pack up and move, God showed me I wasn't supposed to go! As a full-time employee of Liberty University, tuition is free of charge. The Lord opened the door for my student worker position to go full-time! My boss told me that if I would stay and work through the summer, I would be full-time by the fall. I was excited because I loved this school and everything about it! I stayed, and I am not a full-time employee and I am finishing school! It made me realize God is big enough for anything if I just listen and follow His instructions!

Jessica Black is a 24-year-old college student at Liberty University. She is the daughter of a Marine and a pediatric nurse. She has two sisters, six brothers, one brother-in-law, and one niece.

Courtney's Song

By Darcy Blankenhorn

Courtney is a young lady in the youth group I teach at our church. I had seen Courtney in June of that year and then not again until I ran into her and her grandma at Taco Bell a couple of weeks later. I gave her my usual hug and then realized it had caused her to wince. It was then that I noticed she had baseball-sized lumps on her throat. It had been determined that she had an extremely aggressive form of lymphoma. She decided to try the path her Mother had taken with Huntington's disease, which would also hamper the chemotherapy she would now undergo. So the prayers went up for Courtney. It was at the same time I learned of two others, her age, with the same cancer. So I added them as well to my list of concerns.

At about round five of Courtney's treatment for cancer, she insisted her caregiver, her grandma, bring her to youth meetings. As I waited in the foyer for another youth to finish his evening service opening, in she floated. Not a hair on her body and yet as beautiful as anything I had ever seen. I was so humbled that the God of the Universe would grant me such a blessed sight, and yet how could this child be so sick and still carry her with such a beauty? It was then that I realized it was a song, Courtney's Song, the song we saints sing (as a prayer) to carry the feet of those who can't walk.

On my drive home that evening, "Courtney's Song" was written, melody and all, as God would have it. The song was, miraculously carried to Nashville to be orchestrated and later released as a single. In the journey of the song Courtney became more ill and we feared losing her. The other two young ladies both died in November of 2006 within days of each other. But God has a plan and He chose to hear the singers of "Courtney's Song," all the saints who continued to pray. Courtney is now celebrating life as a survivor of cancer. She has been cancer-free for one year and is driving! I am humbled and awestruck at the God of the Universe who hears my song and allows an answer. God is still in the healing business! I know I'll keep singing "Courtney's Song."

Darcy Blankenhorn is the mother of three children and grandmother of five grandchildren. She has been married to her husband for thirty-six years. She is a singer, soloist, and local quartet tenor.

God Has a Plan

Donald L. Boothe, Sr.

In July of 1996 I had my first in a series of heart attacks. I knew at some point I would have to undergo open-heart surgery, but I was very anxious about it.

First, I did not want the doctors to describe the process to me; I just wanted them to do the surgery and not tell me what to expect. Second, I did not want to go to this particular hospital, but because of insurance, I would have to go there. Third, I did not want this particular doctor to do my surgery because I just did not like his method. Fourth, my youngest son was in the Navy stationed in Maine. I wanted him to be home so he could be with his mother during the surgery.

As always, God has a plan, and He will listen to the desires of your heart if you are faithful to Him. As it turned out, my son was discharged from the Navy and was at home. In fact, he was at our house on Saturday afternoon. We were piddling in the back yard when a massive heart attack hit me. With my son's help, my wife and daughter-in-law got me into the back of our van, and with the seats folded down, I lay down. About two to three miles down the road my wife decided she better call 911 because my pain was worsening. Because of the severity of the heart attack, the ambulance driver said he had to go to the nearest hospital (which was the hospital of my choice). After several hours of trying to stabilize me, the doctor decided I had to undergo bypass surgery immediately.

God answered my prayers, my son was home, I got to go to the hospital I wanted, the doctor did not have time to explain to me the procedure, the doctor I did not want to perform the surgery was not on staff at this hospital, thus the doctor I wanted to do the surgery could do it with no problem with insurance.

God is so good He answered my prayers exactly the way I asked.

Donald L. Boothe, Sr., lives in Chunchula, Alabama, with his wife of thirty-nine years, Shelia. They have two sons, eight grandchildren, and two puppies. They are active members of Cottage Hill Baptist Church in Mobile, Alabama.

It All Started with the McKameys

By Dorothy Bowen

It seemed like things just kept happening to me, and it put me in the depths of depression. In 1996, I was in one of those states of mind over the lost of my oldest daughter, who decided to sever her relationship with me. I could hardly do anything to soothe the devastation I felt. This happened in January.

In February, The McKameys were to appear at a church in Louisville, Kentucky. I decided I was going to go. Peg sang, "When the waves are over your head He's under your feet." At that moment, God took that burden away from me and I was able to finally leave it with Him for His will to be done in my life.

Two months later, Eddie Crook called me and asked me to come to Goodlettsville, Tennessee, for a job interview, a new venture with his company. It was the best job I ever had. Working in southern gospel music was pure joy. The Lord had to put this together because I never even applied for that job. God put it in Elaine Wilburn's heart to tell Eddie about me and the help I had been to them at their product table over the years. Then she called me and Eddie called me and I got the job. I never thought I would ever leave Kentucky, but I did. God put my job, my house, and my church home together in a way I never imagined could ever happened. Though I no longer work for Eddie, he and his family are good friends and I enjoy many more southern gospel concerts in Tennessee than there ever were in Kentucky. I will always believe it all started with The McKameys that February.

Dorothy Bowen retired from the federal government at Fort Knox, Kentucky, and now lives in White House, Tennessee. She has two daughters and five grandchildren.

Jesus Took the Wheel

By Rhonda Wright Bray

We can make plans for our lives, but the Lord's plan will prevail. When you feel defeated about your spiritual work, the Lord is getting ready to lift you spiritually higher than you've ever been.

On Wednesday evening, we started out to the Mississippi Quartet Convention. We were scheduled to sing at Corbin Missionary Baptist Church in Corbin, Kentucky.

The pastor told us to remember it was Wednesday, and not to expect a crowd. The church filled and extra chairs were brought in. The singing and testimonies lasted for one hour. The altar was full and three ladies were saved. There was shouting, clapping, and praising all over the church. We were invited to the basement for food and fellowship. They packed a large box with food to go. We are so thankful the Lord laid on their hearts to send food with us, because the Lord knew we would need a supply of food to have on the bus.

At 2 a.m. on Thursday morning, we were driving down I-75 South. Rodney and Carol had gone to sleep. I had lain down and felt a tug on the bus, and then I heard a loud screech. I jumped up and asked Linden, our bus driver, what had happened. He said we have just lost our front wheel. I asked if he was having trouble steering the bus, and he said no. He gently guided our bus to the nearest exit. We decided to go back to bed, everyone but Linden. He sat up all night praying that no one would be injured by our wheel. He was praising the Lord for sparing us. I cried myself to sleep, thanking the Lord for keeping us safe. We did not have to make any calls for help.

At daybreak, a mechanic walked up to the bus and asked if he could help. At the end of our exit ramp was Mark Shackleford Road

Service. He had phoned Denton's Wrecker to haul our bus to Choo Choo Express Bus Garage, which was eight miles from us. He had them on standby, waiting to repair our bus.

It was noon Thursday when we arrived at the garage. Instead of placing our bus inside the garage, they agreed to leave our bus outside so we could live on the bus while it was being repaired. They furnished us with a van to drive so we could find showers. There was another coach being repaired that belonged to a country music band. The lead singer kept walking around our bus with a puzzled look on his face. Linden asked him if something was wrong. He told us his friends had owned a bus like ours, a 1984 MCI 9, and their front wheel had come off while driving, but their bus had flipped and they were killed instantly. He told us the Lord had protected us.

We asked the owner of the shop if they knew someplace we could sing because we were not going to make it to MSQC. Casey, a pastor and bus driver, told us about a truckers' revival.

On Saturday, our bus was repaired. What should have cost us twelve thousand dollars only cost us six thousand. The owners knew the Lord would bless them for their generosity.

We drove to the truck stop. We turned our speakers to the truck parking lot. A trucker walked out of the dark, came to the altar, and prayed to the Lord for forgiveness.

We give the Lord praise and thank Him for everything He has done and will do in 1 Voice Ministry.

Rhonda Wright Bray grew up singing with her whole family. Their group was called The Wright Family, and they sang at local churches and on their local radio station, WRVK 770am in Renfro Valley, Kentucky. Today Bray and her brother, Rodney, have a singing ministry called 1 Voice.

The Buddy

By Cindy D. Brown

I have worked in the same place for almost fourteen years. The people I have worked with have been like my second family. We've seen our kids grow up, and our kids have kids of their own who are making us proud grandparents. In the last two years, my "work family" has begun to retire and leave. My best friend got another job. Our supervisor also retired. I became very depressed.

We had new people come in that "didn't fit in" to my standards. Our new supervisor came in and tried to change everything about us. I became really down.

I wanted a buddy like I had before. I had no one to really talk to and confide in. We had a prayer group within our agency I had emailed and asked for a prayer. I can't begin to tell you how alone I began to feel. I left on a much needed vacation, knowing a new person was being hired while I was gone.

When I returned to my job the following Monday and asked how the new person was doing, my supervisor told me, "I think you will like her. She knows you." The buddy I had prayed for was the new person they had hired. She ended up being a very good friend I had gone to school with.

My supervisor reminded me, "Remember what you wished for before you left?" I honestly couldn't remember. She said, "You wished for a buddy." Suddenly I realized a prayer had been answered.

God does still answer prayers, and He answered one for me. I now have a friend to confide in and am now happy at work again. My new supervisor thought it would be a good idea to have secret pals at work, and guess who I drew to be my secret pal? You got it, my new supervisor. God does have a way of testing us.

Cindy D. Brown lives in Cantonment, Florida. She is fifty-two years old, married, and has two daughters and five grandchildren. In addition to singing and playing the piano at church, she enjoys gardening and working with her music.

God Has the Final Say

By Julia Ann Burns

This story is about answered prayers, but it is also about how God can use even the littlest ones in our lives that He has blessed us with to bring hope and to get us through the darkest hours of our life.

The year 2000 was a very special year for my husband and me as we celebrated the arrival of a son. This event was a realization of a long-awaited dream. In previous years, my husband and I had tried to have a child and even had the joyous news told to us in the year of 1998 that we were expecting. But that joy was soon overshadowed by the sorrow that comes from having a miscarriage. We were elated that we finally had the child we had been dreaming of, but even this joyous event was overshadow with the news that TJ had a heart defect that would require open heart surgery to correct. There were many complications and one was TJ's weight. He was 6 lbs and 9 oz. when he was born, and the doctors wanted him to get up to 8 lbs before the surgery. Due to the type of heart defect TJ had, he did not have the energy to take a bottle so he had to be tube-fed.

Those days were very dark and uncertain for us. Even though we were keeping the faith that God was in control and He had the final say in TJ's survival, there were many times we felt discouraged and were in need of a ray of hope to shine through. God supplied this ray of hope to us from a five-year-old little girl I had the honor of taking care of when she was a baby at the child development center where I worked at the time. Hayley's mother explained to her why she was going to come visit us in the hospital, and before she left Hayley gave her mother a TY beanie stuffed animal named Hope Bear to give to baby TJ. It was actually Hayley's bear, but she wanted TJ to have it because she felt he needed it more than she did. Hope Bear is a bear who is in a kneeling position with eyes closed and paws folded in prayer. It was a perfect reminder for us every time we felt discouraged to lift our hearts to the Lord in prayer.

TJ never reached 8 lbs before his lungs started to show signs of stress, so we had to make the choice of going ahead with the surgery even though he was not at an ideal weight for surgery or trying to give TJ a little more time to gain some more weight. The doctors warned us that this was treading dangerous waters, risking damage to TJ's lungs. My eyes caught Hope Bear and I silently prayed for wisdom and then heard myself asking the doctor, "If this was your child, what would you do?" His reply was that he would go ahead with the surgery. My husband Jeff and I looked at each other and nodded silently to our decision of going ahead with the surgery. We were told afterwards that the doctor discovered TJ's lungs were in worse shape than had been thought, but by a miracle TJ had survived the surgery! Recovery was rocky and we nearly lost TJ several times, but God had given His answer! We praise the Lord for His intervention, grace, and mercy!

Julia Ann Burns lives in Charlotte, North Carolina. She and her husband Jeff have been married since 1989, and they are the Sunday school preschool directors at University Hills Baptist Church, where they are active members.

The Interpreter

By LaVina Burns

Our son-in-law is Dallas Rogers, tenor for the Dixie Echoes. They were performing in Bonifay, Florida, on July 7, 2007, so my daughter and I attended. Shortly after arriving, we observed a deaf man, Bill, without an interpreter. He sat with a couple of friends, but without understanding. Many wonder why a deaf person would go to a southern gospel concert and question it. However, if one pays attention to the message of the songs, the question is answered! There is the hope of heaven and seeing Jesus, and for a deaf person, they know He will be the first to say their name and hear it! Also, just the knowledge that one day they will hear for eternity!

After inquiring about his need for an interpreter, I was able to interpret the message of the gospel for six hours, and you should have seen the continual smile on his countenance. Time and again he nodded in agreement with excitement. After many thank you's, I was blessed to have been used to sing with the group in sign language and spread the gospel!

An interesting fact was Stewart Varnado had allowed any deaf individual to attend the JG Whitfield Homecoming in Pensacola, Florida, on June 23, 2007, free of charge. I had broken my right arm a couple of years ago and have not been able to use it to interpret since. However, I began exercising it to strengthen it so I could interpret at the homecoming. Little did I know God was using that strengthening and experience to enable me to interpret the six hours at Bonifay. God is good all the time!

LaVina Burns is a deaf interpreter and woman's motivational speaker. Her husband of twenty-nine years is Jim, and they reside in Pensacola, Florida. They have one grandchild, Rebecca Michelle Rogers.

In His Time

By Sharon Burrow

I was in my twenty-eighth year of marriage and it was going downhill fast. We were fighting and sleeping in separate rooms. My husband was angry all the time. I kept my faith, knowing that one day God would save him! I prayed for his salvation for fifteen years.

A friend of mine ordered some Bibles, and they were shipped to my work by mistake. I called him to pick them up. He'd been praying for my husband's salvation for years. He asked me if Frank owned a Bible. I said yes. My friend wrote Scripture verses in a Bible and told me to give it to Frank.

I went away on a staff retreat, and my friend who gave the Bible to my husband and my SS teacher visited my husband while I was away. They ministered to him, and he prayed to receive Christ. My friend stated that he'd never seen someone so sincere and real about receiving Christ as Frank was. He called me and told me the good news. I was so excited. The friend I was rooming with and I were in our PJ's, and we danced up and down the halls of the hotel. People thought we were crazy!

My husband called everyone he knew and asked for forgiveness for how he treated them. What joy filled our souls. It was hard the first year, but the Lord restored our marriage. We renewed our thirtieth wedding anniversary vows. Now we've been marriage thirty-five years and we both are active in our church as youth SS teachers. Praise God! He gives you the desires of your heart. Never give up; God doesn't! It's all in God's timing!

Sharon Burrow is an administrative assistant to the church planting department of Greater Orlando Baptist Association, and currently resides in Clermont, Florida.

Gloves from God

By D. A. Callaway

One cold day late in the fall, I was on a highway headed out of the city when I saw a middle-aged woman standing alongside the road. She had no gloves or hat to keep her warm and not much of a jacket either. I stopped to give her a ride. The woman told me how she lived in a rural area, and how she had hitchhiked thirty some miles to town for a doctor's appointment, and was now catching a ride back home. I was going only part of the way, so I let her out at a well-traveled intersection. And since I was on my way to my office, I gave the woman my favorite and only pair of winter gloves. I knew I was going to miss those gloves, but that they went for a worthwhile cause.

Upon arriving at work, I checked the mail. There was a package from a promotional company, and inside the package was a brand new pair of winter gloves. I was and still remain totally amazed.

D. A. Callaway resides in Reeds Spring, Missouri. He is a talent buyer for Silver Dollar City theme park near Branson.

The Silent Killer

By Carolyn Coleman

I always wondered how someone felt when they were told they had cancer. Well, now I know. I was not mad, angry, disappointed, or anything. I was just numb. I was being treated for low blood, had already had two iron infusions, and was still very tired all the time. I was going to the doctor sometimes weekly and biweekly. I had all kind of tests done, but they could not find out why I was anemic. I also had diabetes.

Dr. Miller knew something was wrong; she could not figure out what it was. I was told to go for a CT scan on February 22, 2007. On February 26, I was called and asked to come to her office that day. I was told I had a spot on my kidney, but I needed a second opinion. I called my husband and told him his faith was going to be tested because I had the awful "c" word, cancer.

On February 28, I was told by my surgeon, Dr Brian Hill, my right kidney was ninety-five percent filled with cancer. Two weeks later, after five hours of surgery, my kidney was gone.

My church is a praying church; we support missions. The morning of my surgery, my Pastor, Quinn Evans, talked with our missionary, Justus Banuel, in India. He said he would send word for all of his three hundred churches to pray for me. I lived in Georgia, but I had friends praying for me in Alaska, California, and at all the local churches. Heaven was filled with prayers for me. My doctors prayed for me, and we prayed for them. I was told by one of my doctors that God made me and He knew I was going to face this, and that he had put Dr. Miller in my path.

I know it was through prayer I reached a speedy recovery. I did not have to have chemo or radiation. It was by the grace of God my doctor had me go for a CT scan. I had no pain or anything for me to suspect I had cancer.

Usually by the time cancer is detected, it is too late. I praise God for giving it to me in my kidney; I can live with only one.

Carolyn Coleman has been married to her husband Ronald for ten years. They have one son, two daughters, and one granddaughter. She is a member of Pleasant Grove Baptist church in Hiram, Georgia.

Sorrow Turns to Joy

By Larry Collie

Elizabeth came into this world on June 14, 1990, through a very traumatic and unexpected turn of events in what should have been a "normal" delivery. Her mother suffered a placental abruption prior to giving birth and subsequently almost bled to death. Lizzie, as she is known, was delivered with no detectable signs of life. When we arrived at the hospital and inquired about the baby's condition, we were told they were trying to save our daughter, but that the baby had not survived. But miraculously, a nurse noticed one of Lizzie's legs jerk and immediately began working on her to try to revive her. They managed to resuscitate her and hooked her up to many machines to help her breathe, regulate her heartbeat, etc. For weeks it was touch and go every day to keep her alive. The doctors repeatedly told us they didn't expect her to live, and even if she did, she would be a "vegetable" due to her being so long without oxygen.

During this time there were many tears and prayers for Lizzie, and our faith was tested to the limit. Then our pastor obtained permission from the medical staff to put a small tape player next to Lizzie's head. He told us to record some gospel music and some healing Scriptures on the tape. We did this, and as the tape softly played next to her pillow, she miraculously began to respond almost immediately. Her blood pressure would stabilize and become normal while the tape played, and she became relaxed and calm. Attending nurses told us she was the sickest baby they had ever seen, and she had so many internal problems with her heart, lungs, liver, etc. One Christian nurse told us that in her twelve years with that hospital, she had never known one baby to survive when red blood was detected in a particular tube inserted into the lungs. We have pictures that show red blood in Lizzie's tube, but God had a plan for her and she did not die.

Shortly after we began playing the tape, doctors determined she had a ruptured intestine and air-lifted her to UNC at Chapel Hill, North Carolina, for emergency surgery. She had to wear a colostomy bag for about 8 months, but the surgery was successful and they later reversed the colostomy.

Initially, progress was slow, but today Lizzie is a seventeen-year-old relatively healthy, happy, and vibrant young lady who is loved by everyone she meets. She has mild cerebral palsy, but it does not slow her down much. Lizzie "lives" for going to church and listening to her favorite music, southern gospel. Nothing excites her more than attending a southern gospel concert and hearing groups in person. Many groups have become so blessed by her exuberance during the singing that they bring her on stage while they sing. The Hoppers have done this several times, and while they sang "Shoutin' Time" during one concert, Lizzie took Kim's microphone out of her hand and brought the house down.

Lizzie is truly a special gift from God and blesses everybody who meets her. Many area churches have told us that concerts are never the same when Lizzie is unable to attend. She is one of southern gospel music's greatest fans. The Bible says that "weeping may endure for the night, but joy comes in the morning." Yes…indeed it does!

Larry Collie and his wife, Judy, are grandparents of Lizzie Davis. They live in Williston, South Carolina, where they attend Green Branch P.H. Church.

He Will Make a Way

By Sherri Collie

His blue eyes stared at me. No sounds, just a deep look that softened my heart.

"This just doesn't seem like you, Sherri. Are you sure?"

"Yes, I will work my notice but need to pursue my dreams," I told them. "I start school in a month and want some time to get everything in order. I am looking forward to college and working on something new right now. I am going to go ahead and make some appointments to free up my calendar this week."

Days later, my doctor walked in with his usual grin and handshake, asking me how everything was. "Fine," I responded with a half grin.

"Well, everything looks okay. Let me know if you want to proceed with the medicines we discussed. It may prevent further surgery."

"I am still thinking about it. I am very uneasy about hormones altering an already dysfunctional system. I do want to avoid the knife again, though. I will let you know."

"Good luck with school," he said as the shut the door.

Getting dressed, I noticed several scars and remembered the next surgery would leave me without the hope I so desperately held onto in the past. Hopes of having another "miracle." There were times I would pass other women and think, *That could have been me. Lord, why not me? Wasn't I good enough the first time? I thought I was doing so well.*

I spent so long praying for a healthy child that it didn't seem fair to be greedy. *I received my healthy child years ago. God blessed me and I must move on.*

I spent the following weekend with Sierra, watching her cheer at camp and trying to clear my mind of the doctor's suggestions. *She is beautiful and can more than take up my time. Everything is okay,* I told myself.

Soon stress settled upon me and the rest of the weekend was spent lying down. I didn't feel well, and each day seemed to be getting worse.

I was on the phone with my mom the next evening when she said, "Do you think you may be pregnant?"

"No way, it is just the stress of leaving work and starting school. Sierra is helping me while Neal is at work. I will feel better soon."

"Well, it doesn't hurt to check," she insisted.

"Okay," I said, pacifying her so she would hang up. Afterward, I could not shake what she had said. *God, what is going on?*

There was a knock at the door.

"Mommy, why are you crying?" Sierra asked from behind the door. Her voice was quiet and calming.

"I will be out in a minute, sweetie. Mommy just isn't feeling good. I promise I am okay."

God, are you sure? Can this really be happening?

"Okay, sweet baby boy," I said as I stared back into his blue eyes. Okay indeed. "You are a dream come true. Now let's go wake up sissy."

God made me perfect when everyone said I was broken. He healed me when they said there was no hope. He never left me and was there the whole time, holding my dream next to His heart, even when I let it go.

To my two children, Sierra and Brandon: Never give up on God or your dreams. He will make a way where there is no way. You are proof of that.

Sherri Collie is a wife and mother of two who resides in Nashville, North Carolina.

Our New Home

By Phyllis R. Cooks

In October 2006, my husband Billy got transferred to Indianapolis, which was two hours away from our Hebron, Kentucky, home. Things were going just fine until the holidays came. He was able to get time off for Thanksgiving. I put his plate in the freezer until he was able to come home the following week. I was okay with that, but when Christmas came and he couldn't come home, I was devastated, as this was our first Christmas apart in twelve years.

I told him to look for a house up there. We had been trying to buy a house in Kentucky, but to no avail. So we contacted a real estate agent in Plainfield, Indiana, and she showed us several houses. We immediately fell in love with the home we would later purchase. But that was not where the prayers were be answered. We had prayed and prayed for a home in Kentucky, but to no avail, so we prayed for a home in Indiana.

In January 2007, we met with the real estate agent. We told her we were Christians and she told us she was one as well. This was God working. We found the home that we wanted, and she gave us the name of a mortgage lender. Lo and behold, he was a Christian, too. We explained our situation to him. We gave him our primary information, and the next day he called us to tell us we were approved. Again, this is God working through prayer. We prayed and prayed.

Once all the necessary paperwork was done, we went to sign the loan agreement. The mortgage lender told us the night we called him to give our information to him, he was driving in his car. He pulled over into a parking lot to take down our information, and would you believe the parking lot he pulled into was that of a church! Now if that isn't God working, I don't know what is.

I feel God answered our prayers by putting that man in that parking lot, because when Christians are working, God is working. We got our home, and to this day I tell everyone God answered our prayers by placing the right people in our lives. You see, we weren't meant to have a home in Kentucky like we had wanted because God had other things in mind for us. So I tell people to never ever give up on praying, because just when you least expect it, your prayers will come true. Our prayers were answered, and this year my husband and I will not be apart for Christmas. Glory be to God and all He does for you and me.

Phyllis R. Cooks lives in Camby, Indiana. She is thirty-nine years old and married to Billy. They have a son, Chris.

Confirmed Love of My Daddy and My Father

By Rena Coomer

While there are so many "God moments" I could write about, there is one special moment that left a lasting impression on me. And here it is…

When my parents married, my dad had the hopes of having a boy. After three girls, they gave up. Seven years later, they decided to try one last time. My parents and all of their friends, certain they'd have a boy this time, began purchasing boy toys. Nine months later I arrived…a bouncing baby girl!

As a child, I found the toys that had been purchased for "the boy," but they wouldn't let me play with them and it hurt my feelings. Growing up, I heard the "we wanted a boy" story numerous times. Through the years the enemy placed this seed of doubt in my mind that I was a disappointment to my dad. I didn't share my real feelings with anyone about this. It was a silent pain. I was driven to win Dad's approval by mowing, feeding the cows, etc.—doing "boy" things. I know he loved me, no doubt about that, but I still felt like I was a disappointment.

Fast forward about twenty-five years to Dad's diagnosis of cancer. Dad progressed to "craziness" because of the morphine, and eventually lapsed into silence as he lay on his death bed. I spent his last night with him in the hospital, and I was getting ready to go home for a bit. Dad awoke, speaking rationally for the first time in weeks. He called me over to his bed and smiled and said, "I was never disappointed that you weren't a boy!" After a brief conversation with him, he lapsed back into silence and passed away before I returned to the hospital.

This was clearly a "God moment" because no one else knew of my concern. God cared about me so much, He allowed Dad to become lucid long enough to clear up this issue within me. It was confirmed that my earthly dad loved me for who I was…and also that my Heavenly Father did as well. What a blessing to know that if my heavenly Father cares enough about these small issues to handle them for me, He's handling the big issues as well. God is good!

Rena Coomer is the station/operations manager of a full-time southern gospel radio station, WYGS. She is also a soloist and a minister's wife.

Plain Ol'e Me

By Debbie Corkern

Upon becoming a Christian at age thirty-nine, I had an eagerness to work for the Lord, but I didn't see how that was possible. My life's ambition was to get out of school, get married, and have kids. Now I have this desire but no education to pursue it.

I got my community involved in Operation Christmas Child. I figured most of them could put together one shoebox for a needy child. I didn't know they wouldn't take time to do such a small thing. They just wouldn't take the time to shop for the supplies. Now how could I make a small impact in this world to bring honor and glory to God?

After a few days I thought, "If they won't shop, maybe they would give me money to shop for them," and they did. I had shoeboxes for 100 children the first year, with the most being 468 a couple of years later.

In each box I put a note. "Hello, my name is Debbie Corkern; I live in Louisiana, USA. I work for an electric company, my husband's name is Michael, and he is a barber. I have one son, Dusty. I hope you enjoy your box. I have been praying for you. I don't know you, but Jesus knows your name and where you live. I hope you can write back to me. God bless you. I hope to hear from you soon." I included my contact information if they desired to contact me. I have received letters from several countries.

In 2003 I received a letter from Pastor Tata Victor in Rajahmundry, India, from a girl in his church saying how much she appreciated the box and she had never seen things like this before. Tata and I kept writing and formed a friendship.

In 2005 God laid on my heart to start an orphanage through Tata. Talk about a shock. Plain ol'e me starting an orphanage. "God, this is nuts!" God was persistent… He kept on insisting I do this. I argued, saying I wasn't educated or anything. He said He was going to do it—not me. He just needed willing hands and feet to accomplish His work.

I've wanted to do something to bring honor and glory to God, but this wasn't quite what I meant. An orphanage completely on the other side of the world?

I contacted Tata to get his thoughts. He was so excited; he said he and his wife had been praying for years for a way to start an orphanage. I knew then that God really wanted me to do this.

Tata sent pictures of seventeen children and said it would cost twenty dollars a month to house, educate, feed, and clothe one child. With India being the number one largest Hindu and the third largest Muslim country in the world, they needed to hear about Jesus. CCO would do this; through Tata they would hear about the love of Jesus.

In two years, Corkern Christian Orphanage has 169 children sponsored. We built an orphanage and a church. We now have a sewing center, teaching a trade that costs 100 dollars a month; a free clinic for the village that costs 450 dollars a month; we give rice and veggies to widows and elderly people for 250 dollars a month, and to lepers for another 250; and for 300 dollars a month we help twelve pastors and their families. We don't always receive money for these other missions, but when we do it's exciting.

God told me to start an orphanage, not a business. Every penny is used for what the donator sends it for. All God wants is our hands and feet. He'll do the rest.

Debbie Corkern is forty-seven years old and lives in Franklinton, Louisiana. She has been working at WST Electric for twenty-eight and a half years. She is married with one child. Along with God, she is the co-founder and president of Corkern Christian Orphanage in Andhra Pradesh, India.

There's a Miracle in the Making

By Evelyn Cotner

One evening in 1990, I was burdened about a teenager of seventeen or eighteen who had been badly injured in an auto accident. I had known his mother since 1961, and he had been a customer in a business my husband and I had. I heard his family had been called to the hospital because doctors didn't know if he would make it or not, so I called a friend to pray for this teen, and she prayed over the phone. When I got off the phone, I still had a big burden for him. I didn't know if he was saved or not.

As I went back to the kitchen to finish dishes, I heard a song on the radio I had never heard before. It sounded so pretty, so I went over to listen to it a little closer. The words that were sung at that very time were: "Your prayers have been heard, and the answer's on the way." I was overjoyed because I knew God was telling me He had heard my prayer.

The young man pulled through and went on to get a job after rehabilitation and even got married. I also heard he had gotten saved. He is still around today. I was so happy that I told him and his parents about hearing that song and how God told me He had heard my prayer. I bought the tape, and I have sung it in different churches. Sometimes I will tell the story first, but I find I can't speak because of the tears, so I don't do that too much. But that song was such a blessing to me and it still is.

Evelyn Cotner lives in Huntington, Arkansas, and has been married for almost forty-seven years. She has three children, six grandchildren, and a grandson-in-law. She attends Huntington Assembly of God, where she plays the organ and schedules singers to sing specials. She enjoys listening to southern gospel music.

The Healing Power of God

By Nancy Cranfield

Back in May of 2005 I started getting sick. I had a lot of nausea, vomiting, and a severe pain in my stomach. Unsure of what was causing the problem, I went to the emergency room. They started doing blood work. My white blood cell count was more than twenty-six thousand. They immediately admitted me to the hospital and started running tests.

My husband, in the meantime, had to contact our pastor, and other people of our church all began praying. The doctors thought I had a problem known has acid reflux disease. That diagnosis was proven incorrect. I continued to grow even sicker. We kept on having people pray, and I was getting weaker.

I eventually became so weak that by January of 2006 I had to take medical leave from my job. My doctors continued to run tests. I was placed on a feeding tube due to the weight loss and the fact that I was unable to keep food down. My veins collapsed, and I had to have a port cath put in. It got to the point were I was in bed most of the time because I was so weak. If I got up, I was on a walker.

The doctors finally diagnosed me as having a rare disorder called gastroperieses. This is where the stomach muscles become paralyzed. Everyone continued praying for me, and my husband continued keeping people up to date on my condition. Little did I know that over the next several months I would lose more than fifty pounds in weight. I was continuing to lose weight so badly that the doctors to decided to put a feeding tube in permanently. The doctors wanted me to come back that following Sunday for the feeding tube to be placed.

When I went to the hospital that Sunday, I and my husband had been praying, and so had the people at our church and other friends of ours. I was taken back to the holding area to be prepped for the surgery and then on to the operating room where my doctor was going to do the surgery. My doctor came in and asked how I was doing. I told him I had been able to get some food down the day before. God came down and just spoke peace and said, "You're not going to have to have this tube at all." My doctor told me we could hold off on doing the feeding tube if I wanted to and do it later if necessary. It was great. I started feeling so much better.

The operating room people wheeled me back into the recovery room, and for the first time in months I was able to get up off a stretcher and walk out of the hospital on my own. I know that was God. The doctors had told my husband several months back I would never work again. In February of 2007 I went back to work. I feel wonderful. I know that it was the healing power of God that brought me through it all. I truly praise Him for everything.

Nancy Cranfield is forty-two years old and lives in Athens, Tennessee. She is a nurse who works with the mentally challenged. She and her husband attend Athens Free Saints True Holiness Church.

Family Forever

By Lanette Currie

Being an early childhood special education teacher was not just her profession, but her calling. With the summers off, she was able to spend a couple summers on missions in Lithuania. The children were very dear to her and tugged at her heart.

Her desire to adopt a little girl to share her life with continued to grow. She prayed daily and felt God had truly placed this desire in her heart. As her mother, I did have some concerns. My daughter was single, and I knew this would not be easy for a single mom. But I also knew she had a strong faith in God.

She called me one day and said, "Mom, I backed God in a corner today."

"What do you mean?" I asked.

She said she had told God, "If this is something You really want me to do, I need a sign. I need You to open some doors." She knew it would be difficult to do alone, without God's help.

Within days of her plea to God, she was driving home from school and received a call from her agency. They had something they wanted her to see and asked if she could come by.

As she left the agency, she called me and was so overjoyed. "Mom," she said, "I got my sign. God opened the door and I have a precious little girl!"

All of this happened within a couple months after she completed the paperwork. Her home study had just started. She had bought a house the year before and had used much of her savings. She worked a second job through Christmas and weekends, saving all her earnings to pay the fees and travel to China to bring her little girl home. She even did some fundraisers along with her friends and her church. Through God's miraculous love, all the expenses were more than met.

Mama and daughter recently celebrated their first year together as "family forever." How overwhelming that God would choose our family to bless with the love of this precious little child.

Our little "princess" has undergone palate surgery and is facing a couple more surgeries in the future. She loves her church and learning about Jesus. She loves singing with the praise and worship team and doesn't want to leave for children's church until the last song has been sung. At Easter, I answered my phone and heard a little voice say, "Grandma, Jesus alive, yeah!"

God did such a perfect job putting these two together, and He is still performing miracles in their lives every day. I believe He is saying, "I spoke and you listened. Well done, my good and faithful servant!"

Lanette Currie is a sixty-year-old grandmother to a little Chinese girl, Hannah. She lives in Rocky Face, Georgia, with her husband and works as an office manager for an internal medicine doctor in nearby Dalton. Hannah lives in Alabaster, Alabama, with her mom, DeEtte.

Premature Twins

By Sandra Dale

My grandsons, Isaac and Jacob Little, were born three months early on December 9, 2005 in Wilmington, North Carolina, at New Hanover Regional Medical Center. Isaac weighed 1 lb. 13 oz and Jacob weighed 1 lb. 10 oz. Isaac suffered a grade 4 brain bleed on Sunday, December 11, 2005 and wasn't expected to live through the night.

During their long NICU stay, they suffered through many infections, surgeries, and setbacks we were told to expect. Yes, we expected all these things to happen, but we also knew we had a great Physician who had it all under control!

Jacob was discharged from the NICU on March 13, 2006. Isaac was flown to Duke University Medical Center on this same date because of a severe infection. He had a shunt placed to help drain the excess fluid that built up because of the brain bleed, and he also had a feeding tube inserted.

After many, many prayers on his behalf by Christians all over the world, he was discharged on July 5, 2006. As of today, Isaac still has the shunt, and still has the feeding tube, but he is able to eat baby food, cookies, etc. He will keep the tube until he's able to sustain himself on food and liquids.

We know the day is coming when he will be able to do this on his own. Even after all this, he is doing better than the doctors had expected. Jacob has far exceeded the doctor's expectations. He is walking and doing all the normal things an eighteen-month-old should do. We know that if God had not intervened and performed the miracles in their lives, things would have been a lot different today. Thanks to God for these two miracles!

Sandra Dale is married with three children and seven grandchildren. She currently resides in Delco, North Carolina.

Cancer Led Me to
Southern Gospel Music

By Douglas A. Drake

In 2004 I was diagnosed with prostate cancer. My urologist, a Christian, found cancer in a biopsy. One positive sample did not qualify me for further tests or treatment. I had a second procedure. This time, there were no positive results. Prayer answered—well, not really. My doctor, Dr. Robert Sewell, said I needed close monitoring until he felt sure all was well. Dr. Sewell knew financially we were exhausted, and was graceful in working with us on payments.

At this time, with the possibility of cancer lingering overhead, I discovered southern gospel radio. I settled on southern gospel radio—there was no theology to disagree with, just positive, uplifting music from artists such as the Dove Brothers, Brian Free and Assurance, and Squire Parsons. I even began to attend southern gospel concerts at a local church.

The power of Jesus Christ and southern gospel music kept me uplifted for one year. Then Dr. Sewell found cancer again; this time it qualified for treatment. I listened to southern gospel as I traveled for my job, and after my surgery I listened to it on the Internet while I recovered.

Six months after my surgery, a coworker dropped a four hundred-pound piece of equipment on me and crushed my leg. The uplifting sound of southern gospel music and the power of prayer kept me going. Now I had two burdens: recovering from cancer and hoping it stayed gone, and struggling with leg problems. Southern gospel kept my spirits up.

Four months after getting my leg crushed, My wife left me. I started leaning on Jesus literally because of the leg injury, and now the abandonment by my wife. It was just me and Jesus, southern gospel music, and my dog. Two months after my wife left, my dog died.

Well, that was about as low as one could get. My faith and constant reassurance from southern gospel music helped me through. Well-meaning friends sometimes help, and sometimes they make things worse, but the gospel message in the form of a positive song and prayer keep me going.

Douglas A. Drake lives in White House, Tennessee, and works as an ICEE repairman.

Out of a Job

By Downing Jeffrey Duncan

In September 2005, I suddenly found myself out of a job. A job I liked, was good at, and had performed faithfully and, for most of my 21-year career, with little or no supervision. The reason: excessive absenteeism due to declining health.

I had been transferred from Rome, Georgia, to Atlanta during July of 1998, and I chose not to relocate to Atlanta, a decision that left me with a drive of about one hour and forty-five minutes one way. During the summer of 1998, and a few months into 1999, I was doing fairly well. I was able to work some overtime and make a few new friends, and I realized the transfer I had dreaded so much maybe wasn't going to be so bad after all.

Then my health started to decline. I had kidney stones, Fibromyalgia, arthritis, high blood pressure, migraine headaches, and eventually degenerative disks in my back. With each passing year, I missed more and more work, until finally my employer terminated me.

I had been talking with my sister about how I could get out of Atlanta, and still be able to make a decent living, and we decided we should be in prayer about it. Then the hammer fell on my job and my 21-year career was suddenly at an end. I had little time remaining for insurance coverage, after which I would have to pay for it myself under the COBRA plan. As I broke the news of my termination to her, she suggested we look at it as God working in my life, rather than me receiving an unfair break from my employer. So that is what we did. I found myself in prayer, asking God to work in my life, and to help me not to ever doubt His hand was on my life.

Music is a tremendous part of my life. I am not very talented myself, but that has never hindered my enjoyment of music. I had been listening to contemporary Christian and praise and worship music for most of the past ten years, and my sister had shared her favorite southern gospel artists with me, and in addition to that, I would play my favorite piano pieces almost every day if my back would allow me to.

Then, because of the lengthy time process of getting a disability decision, I had to sell my piano, but I didn't let it get me down. Instead, I looked at it as a minor setback.

It was around this time that my sister had turned me on to Karen Peck and New River and Greater Vision, and I had been watching the Gaither Homecoming videos for years. Sis brought me a compact disc of Karen Peck's one day and said, "You won't find a better CD than this one." She was right on the money with that statement, and I found myself listening to it every day in addition to another CD that had my all-time favorite Four Days Late on it. The CD she had given me had great songs on it from start to finish, but those that ministered most to me were "He's Sending Miracles," "God Likes to Work," and "God Still Answers Prayer." I listened to "He's Sending Miracles" at least once each day, followed by a prayer that He would work a miracle for me.

God did see me through those trying times, thanks to encouragement from friends, prayer, help from my church, and some very good gospel music. Praise the Lord!

Downing Jeffrey Duncan lives in Rome, Georgia. He is currently disabled, and is a novice songwriter, having completed two or three songs and about seven choruses thus far.

The Wall of Prayer

By Sharon C. Dyer

In February of 1999, my mother-in-law and I went to hear The McKameys in concert in Rome, Georgia. It was just the three of us—Betty, myself, and the Lord. We absolutely loved The McKameys—their songs, which were filled with the Word of the Lord, and their sweet spirit. I was very happy to be there at the concert, but I was thinking of my mother. She was in very bad health and living with my sister in North Carolina.

Then Peg started talking about their new song, "The Wall of Prayer," and the prayer requests they were receiving from their followers and fans. While they sang this song, my heart was filled with the Lord's touch. When they finished this song, they told all of us that if we had someone in our heart we wanted to be touched through prayer, to write down their name and they would insert the request into the wall they had in Tennessee. Well, I did just that. And it was like the Lord was telling me my mother would be fine in a few weeks.

Three weeks later, o March 12, the Lord called my mother home to be with Him. Praise His holy name. What a wonderful day the concert was and the homecoming my mother had. Thank you, Peg, for your commitment to our wonderful Christ.

Sharon C. Dyer lives in Dalton, Georgia. She has been married for thirty-one years to her husband. They have a son, a daughter-in-law, and a grandson. They all attend Eleventh Avenue Baptist Church.

I Believe in Miracles

By Debra Fender

M y story begins about one year ago in May 2006. We were having church one Sunday evening when the Lord graced us with a prophecy. I don't know exactly everything that was told, but I do know the impact it had on all of our lives. The main point of the prophecy was that not many days from now our little church could expect to go through some very trying times, but He promised He would see us through it all the way to the end!

My brother-in-law, the pastor of our church, and his wife worked at the boy's ranch in Hahira, Georgia, and were required to take their boys on vacation during the summer. That year they chose to visit Orlando and some of the theme parks there.

Shortly after departing, they stopped in Gainesville because Jimmy was not feeling well. Louise asked him if he needed to go to a hospital, but he said no. This was the first heart attack.

They traveled to their destination and went to get dinner. After dinner they went to bed. At about midnight jimmy woke Louise and told her he thought he was having a heart attack. This was the second attack.

She immediately called the paramedics. When they arrived, they said he was having an attack. That was number three. They transported him immediately to the hospital and swiftly proceeded to take care of him. Orlando had one of the foremost hospitals for cardiac care in the nation! I believe God allowed him to get to Orlando for this reason.

Within one hour, he was in intensive care after the doctors had put in stints to open the blockage of ninety percent of his heart. Louise called my husband and me to come to Orlando and also to pray for

Jimmy. I immediately called church members and asked them to pray. This was at about 2:00 a.m.

By 5:30 we arrived in Orlando. Jimmy was alert, but he never realized how bad this really was. He only gave God the glory for seeing him through this trial. We all recalled the warning God had given us and thanked Him for the knowledge.

Jimmy was discharged about one week later and went home. In the meantime, the church prayed that the Lord would not only help and watch over Jimmy but also create a new heart for him, better than the repaired one he had.

Jimmy went in for his six-month check-up when the doctor told him that he had had a severe heart attack, but he was totally amazed at the findings. There was no blockage, no scar tissue. In his words, "It's like you have a completely new heart!"

God answers prayers when you pray earnestly. I give Him all the glory and honor for this miracle. As for the rest of us, we are all going through some tough things in our lives, but God is seeing us through as He promised. Nothing is impossible with God!

Debra Fender is a 51-year-old mother of four and grandmother of five living in Ray City, Georgia.

Aaron's Cross

By John Finney

A nineteen-year-old young man named Aaron Eason was driving home to his parents' house in Burkeville, Virginia, on Monday, April 9, 2007, when he was instantly killed in a horrible accident. He was going to stop by the house quickly and then head to the hospital in Farmville where his brother Adam and Adam's wife Kimberly were in the process of giving birth to their first child. Just before the birth, Adam ducked out of the delivery room for a second to tell his mom, dad, and in-laws who were patiently waiting outside the delivery room that he thought it was a girl. Adam looked at the clock on the wall in the delivery room when the baby finally came, and it was 5:55 p.m., as pronounced by the doctor at the time of birth. Just seconds after the birth, Adam's wife asked Adam if he could see the angel, pointing to the convex delivery room mirror. She asked him more than once about this, but so much was happening, and he was so overcome with emotion that it all ran together at the time. He quickly returned to the task at hand and helped deliver his and Kimberly's new baby girl. A short time later he returned to the waiting room only to learn that his brother had died within minutes of the baby's birth. Aaron's last cell phone activity was 5:53 p.m.

The next few days, needless to say, were tough on the family. Can you imagine the emotional swing from pure joy at the birth of a new precious life, to great loss due to the sudden tragic death of a son and brother? The Easons are a family of faith, pillars in our church, and have loved the Lord all the days I have known them. However, this was a real test of their faith.

Aaron's dad, Jack, was distraught, and two days later he could not stand it any longer. He retrieved his handgun and contemplated ending his life. He had prayed to God, asking Him, "Did my sin cause this? Is this in any way my fault?" He asked God for a sign, something he could hold on to that would indicate to him his son was spiritually okay. You see, Aaron had been going the way I did when I was his age, as I'm sure many of you reading this did, too. He had been brought up in church, but he was delving in some things that concerned his parents. So Jack was crying out to God because he had to be sure that Aaron's commitment to Christ years ago was real, and that he was in fact in heaven. So with gun in hand, he had already decided that if God did not give him the answer he needed, he would end it all. Fortunately, he put the gun away and continued on in his grief.

Later, the family went to the funeral home to make final arrangements for Aaron's burial. It was there that Paul, our pastor, asked Jack if he had seen the cross. At the accident site, Paul had seen up in the tree over the point of impact a cross made by two pieces of tree bark that had obviously been jarred loose from the impact. When Jack and the family heard this, they all left the funeral home immediately and went to see this cross. There, Jack, Adam, Wynona, and Kimberly jumped out of the car, and while gazing upon this obvious sign from heaven, the woods resounded with their sobs of grief and joy. Yes, joy, because now they knew Aaron was safe in the arms of God. This was on Tuesday, the day after the accident. On Wednesday, the cross fell out of the tree while Jack was pointing it out to the out-of-town family members who had just arrived from North Carolina.

John Finney currently resides in Amelia, Virginia.

My Miracle

By Kimberly Franks

I had to go to the doctor because of severe pain in my lower back, and he told me I had a bad kidney infection. I told him my back hurt and there was a knot on it. He felt it and said he didn't like the way it felt. He said it was a cyst that was the size of my fist. He was already setting it up for me to be put into the hospital, to have something done about it.

I went home and told my family what the doctor told me. Then I went to lie down for a little bit.

My parents were going to a sing/revival that night to see a group we had heard on the radio, and they asked me if I wanted to go. I said no because I was hurting so bad I couldn't even sit still.

I decided right at the last minute to go. But I didn't even enjoy it because I couldn't sit still through the whole service. I was hurting so badly. I didn't even pay attention to the singing or the preaching, which was totally unlike me.

When it came time for the invitation, my mom asked me if I wanted to go up and have the preachers pray over me. I said no because I could hardly stand up, and I knew I wouldn't be able to last up there standing up that long.

As we were walking toward the door, my dad told the visiting preacher (the one who had done the service) that "we enjoyed the service, and please keep my daughter in your prayers." He told the preacher what I had found out that morning at the doctor's office.

It was taking every single bit of strength and willpower for me to stand up there. The preacher looked at me, and said, "We'll pray for her right now." He called the church's preacher over, and I don't even know who else, and they all laid hands on me and started praying.

My dad said he was watching me. He knew right when my "miracle" took place. He said he saw it in my eyes.

When the preacher finished his prayer, I hugged him and said thank you. By the time I walked out the door, I was no longer in pain. By the time I got home ten minutes later, that mass was completely gone!

I went back to the doctor, and he said he could find no trace of that cyst whatsoever. He asked me what happened, and I told him how I had been prayed over. He told me that nothing he could have done could have matched the healing power of the Lord.

I have not had any trouble with it ever since!

Kimberly Franks is the youngest of three girls. She lives in Branford, Florida, with her family and two dogs. She works at Fort White High School in the cafeteria as a support aide.

Only God Knew

By Mandy Freeman

I have been a preacher's daughter all my life. Growing up in church for twenty-four years, I've heard countless stories about the power of prayer. But I never truly experienced that power until May of 2002.

My dad, Bruce Freeman, is the pastor of Peace Haven Baptist Church in Yadkinville, North Carolina. For twenty-eight years he has preached about our powerful God and how He is faithful to answer our prayers. God tells us in His Word, "Call unto me and I will answer thee, and shew thee great and mighty things, which thou knowest not" (Jeremiah 33:3). Our family had no idea of the test we would face and how we would see that promise come true in our lives; only God knew.

It was Thursday, May 9, and my dad had gone to the church to change the light bulbs in some of the main sanctuary lights. Our church sanctuary is large, and the ceiling reaches about forty-five feet in height. Several times, Dad had used a powered lift to reach the lights.

That night, when the lift was at full extension, it began to sway. The lift fell backwards, toward the stage, carrying my Dad thirty-five feet downward to the concrete floor. He told us he knew the steps of the stage were behind him, and there was nothing he could do but tell our family goodbye and wake up in glory. Mike, a deacon of our church who was helping Dad that evening, immediately called 911.

Mike called and told us to get to the church; the lift had fallen with Dad in it. We found Dad lying at the base of the stage, crying out in pain, his legs twisted in the lift. In just moments, the rescue squads arrived and emergency personnel rushed to get Dad to the hospital. They knew his injuries were serious. As we followed the rescue squad down the road, all we could do was call out to God to spare his life and begin to heal his body.

In the first few hours at the ER, the doctors were preparing us for the worst. Dad would most likely never walk again. He had a shattered right pelvis and broken arm, and would be in the hospital for months. This was their diagnosis. God had other plans. You see, back home in Yadkinville, several of our church members had already begun to pray for their pastor. Many of them met at the church and cried out to God to spare their pastor and bring healing to his body. For the next several months, thousands of people prayed for my dad and his recovery.

The doctors said most people who fall that far never survive; only God knew He wasn't finished with my dad yet. They said the nerve damage in his left leg would never heal; only God knew those nerves still had life in them. Today, Dad walks without the help of crutches or a cane. We questioned whether or not Dad would ever preach again; only God knew that in August of that year, Dad would return to the pulpit! As the Bible said, we called out to God, and He showed us great and mighty things!

How did my Dad survive that fall that day? What really went on inside his body after the fall? How many prayers were heard and answered for my Dad that day? Only God knew.

Mandy Freeman is twenty-four years old and lives in Clemmons, North Carolina, with her parents, Pastor Bruce and Cindy, and one sister, Marsha. She enjoys Bible preaching and gospel music.

Through the Tough Days

By Anna Gardner

I grew up in a pastor's home, a good Christian home. Life was going great. We had just moved from South Carolina back home, and we were all excited!

My dad accepted a call from one of the largest churches in the area to be their pastor. We were thinking this would all be great. We entered a new building program and had the new church built within the year. We had a big grand opening and it went great!

But things I did not understand had been happening with my dad along the way. Little did I know that two weeks after we got into the new building my dad would walk out of the ministry and away from our family. Quit everything. That was probably the hardest thing in my life. I could have never imagined in a million years that I would be standing where I was! I knew God was in control and that what the enemy had meant for evil God would use for His good.

Twenty-three years later during the very same month my dad had walked away from the ministry, the Lord opened a door for me to walk into ministry. I was eighteen at the time; I played the piano and sang. I remember it like yesterday. I received a phone call from a friend who knew nothing of my situation. She asked, "Anna, would you consider filling in or traveling with Second Coming full-time?" I couldn't believe it; just when I thought my life was over God stepped in with a plan, His plan. A plan to prosper me and give me hope. Do I think this was just an accident or a coincidence? No, I don't. I believe God will use anything He allows to happen to you for His glory.

I am in my second year singing with "Second Coming". The awesome thing about God is that He knows the end when we can't see an end. I have seen God move in my life more over the last year than any other time before. He has become so much sweeter to me, and I know He will truly use any life that is fully surrendered to Him in the good times and the bad times... He's still God.

Anna Gardner lives in Newnan, Georgia. She is nineteen and enjoys southern gospel music, singing, and playing the piano.

God's in the Business of Answering Prayers

By Stan Garner

I'll never forget the day we dropped him off in Soso, Mississippi, at the age of eighteen. What a long ride back to Southern Illinois. Friends, that's a long way to drive teary-eyed! We asked the Lord to at least give him five years to plant himself in the industry.

Well, the prayer was answered, and God Himself placed our son, Josh, with one of the most respected names in the southern gospel music industry. It was such an honor to be able to travel with Les, Glen, Darrell, and Gene. Words cannot describe the learning experience that one can achieve by traveling with such great men in this industry. To be able to stand beside these godly men as they go into retirement is such a thrilling experience!

Les, Glen, and Darrell will always be known as the legendary Florida Boys. These men have become family of ours and will always be. I wish every young man going into this field would have the opportunity to at least spend one week with Glen Allred. God has used this man in a special way, and he would be a perfect example for every young man going into this field!

I praise God, for this answered prayer, for allowing our son to be a part of this great history in southern gospel music!

Stan Garner currently resides in Fairfield, Illinois. He and his wife Marti are the parents of Joshua Garner of the legendary Florida Boys. The family sang for many years with the Cavalrymen Quartet, then they formed The Garner Boys Quartet in 1991 and sang together until 1997, when Josh moved on to be with The Florida Boys.

I Continue to Sing Because of His Awesome Power

By Greg Gaston

On February 28, 2006, I went to my doctor with major abdominal pain. He wasn't sure what the problem was, but he sent me down the hall to a surgeon. Here is where I know God stepped in and took charge.

Dr. Richard Perry was his name, and I am thankful he was so gifted and a man of God. He not only happened to be in his office at the time, but within thirty seconds he diagnosed me with a rare disease called Meckel's Diverticulum. Only one percent of the population has this genetic disease, and of that one percent, only one percent develops any major complications.

He immediately rushed me to the hospital, and four hours later I had the first of four surgeries to fix the problem. If he hadn't diagnosed me correctly and operated as he did, I would not be still sharing God's love through music. God put Dr. Perry in my path and showed me He is and always will be my source of power as I minister to others with Gaston Ministries and share His love through music.

As the son of a minister, Greg Gaston knew at an early age he was to sing God's music and share His love with others. In 1994, at the age of forty-seven, he dedicated his life to His call. He shares God's music in Phoenix and around the state of Arizona in care centers and churches.

My Answered Prayer

By Dottie Gill-Bonds

In May of 2006 my older sister decided to retire and move back to Louisiana. She and her husband had been living in Florida for many years. So, arrangements were made and I caught the Greyhound bus and rode down to Pensacola.

All the next day was spent loading up the rental truck, and that night we checked into a motel. Early the next morning I slipped out to the truck. I began to walk all around the truck and trailer that had their car on it and pray. "Lord Jesus, I love You. And I am asking You, Lord, to protect us on our journey. Please, please, Lord, let us have a safe journey with no breakdowns or accidents. Lord, I love You and I know You will be with us on this journey."

Well, we hit the road. My sister, her husband, four cats in carriers, and I were all in the cab of the truck. My sister was afraid to try to drive the truck and my brother-in-law was legally blind. So, off we went. It was quite a ways to Natchitoches Parish, Louisiana, from Florida. I told them we would not push it and we might have to stop for the night.

Several times on our journey I noticed that the truck did not seem to want to pull hills, but it just kept on going. We stopped several times for fuel and just to walk around. Around 4 p.m. we were going through Alexandria, Louisiana, on Interstate 49. This was just an hour or so from home, so I called my pastor on my cell phone and asked if he could get some of the church family to come help us unload the truck. We were making excellent time.

We rolled off the interstate onto Highway 120 and proceeded onward to Provencal. We rolled through town, with me pointing out the sights. I turned left into the park where I had found them a home

70

to rent and the engine was running, but the truck would not move. We were three hundred feet from their house where I could see my best friend waiting for me.

People began to come up to the truck, and my sister kept saying "Who are these people?" I kept assuring her they were church members.

It turns out the accelerator cable had broken. My friends were able to get the truck to move with a temporary repair. In just a couple of hours they had the car off the trailer and the truck unloaded. The next day a mechanic came to check out the truck. He was amazed it had made it so far with all its problems. He just could not believe we made it so far in such a wreck of a vehicle. I told him I know who holds tomorrow and I know who holds my hand. When I told him about my circle of prayer around the vehicle before we left, he just smiled and said prayers are always answered.

He will never leave us or forsake us. All we have to do is ask and we will receive.

Dottie Gill-Bonds is a mother, sister, and grandmother. She retired from AT&T and now works in a school as a custodian. She currently lives in Provencal, Louisiana.

His Blessing on Me

By Dr. Wayne Alvin Gooden

Like most Americans, I know exactly where I was on September 11, 2001. I was on duty at the Pentagon as a federal police officer. Instead of eating breakfast that morning, I was outside talking with my daughter Donnie about the attacks on the World Trade Center.

Right after I hung up my cell phone, the plane hit the Pentagon. God saved my life that day, because if I was inside eating breakfast in the area where the plane hit, I might not be here today. Each day I thank God for saving my life on 9/11.

On Father's Day 2004, I began singing gospel music again. This is my way of showing God how grateful I am for His saving my life not only on 9/11, but also from two vehicle accidents where each vehicle was totaled, and in Vietnam.

On September 9 and 11, 2006, along with other gospel singers, I hosted a 9/11 Memorial Concert at Fort Gordon, Georgia. I will be hosting a 9/11 2007 Memorial Concert this year as well, and I am planning on going to the Pentagon on September 24 for the memorial concert there. Along with some other gospel singers, I hosted a gospel concert last year on June 16 at the Pentagon.

Each day I wake up and say, "Thank You, Lord." I have recorded two CDs, and on the first recording, the song "Thank You, Lord, For Your Blessing on Me," was rewritten by Russell Easter, Sr., of the Easter Brothers. The song was about how God saved my life at the Pentagon.

Dr. Wayne Alvin Gooden began his singing career at the age of five. Sixty years later, he is still singing with the New Beginning Gospel Music ministry. He is a member of the Police Officer's Ministries Association, the

North Carolina Gospel Music Association, and the Southern Gospel Music Association. He currently resides in Hephzibah, Georgia.

My Pastor, the Miracle Man

By Tabetha Greene

In March 2007, my pastor, 61-year-old Delmont "Seven" Gibson, was diagnosed with a tumor on his brain. It was not cancer. His mind had been gradually getting worse before and even after they found out. But he didn't give up!

On April 3, 2007, he was scheduled to have the baseball-sized tumor removed. He went in that morning, and they did tests to make sure he could have this serious brain surgery. Well, his blood glucose level was unbelievably high, so they couldn't do the surgery. They kept him a whole week and on April 9, they continued with the surgery.

Around fifty to sixty people, both family and friends, waited in the waiting room. They took him in for surgery at about 9 a.m. and finished around 4:30 p.m. The doctor came out and told his wife and two grown children he made it through the surgery and was in recovery. We had prayer and rejoiced that he was going to be all right. His wife and children was finally able to see him around 8:30 that night.

On Friday, April 13, he was doing so well they let him come home from the hospital. About another month and he was back to preaching. He later told us that while he was in surgery, he was crossing death's river. He said he was fighting those waves so hard and finally he just gave up and lay back, and the waves pushed him back to life. His wife said that was all the prayers bringing him back to us.

That's a miracle and a blessing from God! We are still so fortunate to have him with us today! Everyone now calls him "The Miracle Man."

Tabetha Greene is eighteen years old. She was saved March 21, 2007, and baptized on July 1, 2007. She attends ELM Springs Baptist Church in Sneedville, Tennessee.

A Tremendous Blessing

By Margaret Rose Griffin

The story of my angelic encounter happened thirty-six years ago, but it still brings me hope, peace, and confidence in God's amazing grace.

My two-year-old asthmatic daughter, Karen, had just returned home from Campbellord Ontario Memorial Hospital after a three-day stay in the croupette, as the result of an acute asthma attack. The doctor had reluctantly released her at 3:00 p.m. but said her oxygen levels were still too low and I should return to the hospital if her breathing became more distressed.

After nursing her brother and tucking him in bed for the night, I bathed our beautiful little blond-haired girl and listened to her gasping wheeze and watched her painful struggle to breathe. It was 7 p.m., and I knew my church would be praying for her during their evening service.

Seeing her suffer so, I realized I would have to return to the hospital and that I should go before the afternoon shift went off duty. Her fresh pink cotton pajamas were already damp with perspiration and her little fingernails were turning blue.

I took a minute to sit in the rocking chair in Karen's bedroom with her fragile body draped limply over my shoulder. As I gently rocked her, I thanked God for giving us this precious little girl. She had such a vibrant, enthusiastic personality and she learned so quickly. I acknowledged that she was only on loan to us from her loving heavenly Father, and I asked for the wisdom to deal with her severe asthma.

It was exactly 7:20 p.m. on her little lamb dresser clock when her dark bedroom was flooded with a bright light. This pillar of light was in the corner of her soft pink bedroom and my precocious two-year-old said, "Mommy, where did that light come from?"

It was then that I heard a voice assuring me my baby girl was going to be fine and she would grow up to be a tremendous blessing to everyone whose life she would touch.

As the light faded away, I realized my daughter was not wheezing anymore. Her breathing was normal, her fingernails and toenails had returned to a healthy pink shade, and she wanted to go to sleep.

Was the light an angel bringing healing, encouragement, and peace? Was the light the angel of death who knew this was not God's chosen time for Karen to depart? Why did God choose this little, insignificant family to pour out His grace and love?

Whatever, or whoever, spoke to me that night made an absolutely right prediction. My 38-year-old daughter is a tremendous blessing to our family. As I enter into a battle with breast cancer, my daughter is right there, fixing meals, buying me health food supplements, and managing my wardrobe. Best of all, my daughter, her husband, and her two wonderful sons are our faithful prayer warriors and uphold our whole family through prayer.

Since that Sunday evening thirty-six years ago, I have experienced God's ministering angels in many ways—through nurses, surgeons, lab and x-ray technologists, pastors, and a whole army of faithful friends. Never again have I experienced an unusual divine intervention, but I shall always praise God for His faithfulness and love through ministering angels.

Margaret Rose Griffin and her husband of forty-five years, Bill, have been promoters of music for more than thirty years. They reside in Calgary, Alberta, Canada, and have two grown children and two grandchildren.

He Brought Me Through

By Elaine Harcourt

I had been let go of the job I had and needed. What was I to do? I turned on my radio and The Kingsmen were singing "You're Not Alone." I knew somehow God was going to take care of me.

I began putting in my résumé and going on interviews. I was past fifty—who was going to take a chance on me? On top of that, I had a persistent cold and wasn't making the best presentation.

I went for an interview with an architectural company. When I was asked why I had left my previous job, I told them the truth. It didn't work out and I had been let go. No point in lying. I thought, *Well, that's it!* The next day they called me and hired me! I had only been out of work ten days! Praise God; He brought me through again!

Elaine Harcourt lives in Wichita, Kansas, and works as a receptionist for an architectural firm. She is a 65-year-old widow and lives alone with her cat. She has five grown kids, ten grandkids, and two great-grandkids. She loves southern gospel music.

Product of Prayer

By K.K. Edgil Hargett

November 28, 2003 was our annual Thanksgiving Sing in Florence and the first one I had missed in twenty years. The reason I had missed it was because I was sick.

On November 29, I was admitted to Huntsville Hospital, where I stayed for almost three moths. I was on a ventilator for three months and was in the hospital a total of four months.

On November 28, thousands of people began to pray for me and for my healing. My family was told I would not make it, but I did. The Hoppers, the Kingsmen, the Perry's, and countless others began to pray on my behalf. The doctors said I might never walk again, and if I did, it would be years before I could. After ten months, I was out of my wheelchair, my feeding tube was gone, and I grew stronger each day. I know it was because of those prayers that I am here today and can share with others the wonderful grace of God.

K.K. Edgil Hargett currently resides in Muscle Shoals, Alabama.

An On Time God

By James R. Harris

On July 30, 2004, my youngest niece was born. Not long after, my brother and sister-in-law took her for her one-week check-up. Well, just two or three days before this they noticed her leg twitching, so when they took her for her check-up the doctor told them she had a light case of epilepsy. He put her on some medicine, and they did some tests and said they found a spot on her brain—she'd had a stroke.

In a few months they did some more tests and said they found another spot on her brain and she'd had another stroke. When they said she had epilepsy, my brother and sister-in-law had their church pray for her. They called us to have us pray, and we had a church in Harrison, Arkansas, praying for her as well. The doctors kept checking up on my niece, and through this all we were trusting in God.

Finally, they began to cut her medicine dosages down little by little. When my brother and sister-in-law were home in March 2007, we were all down at my grandparents' house. One of my uncles asked my sister-in-law how Reagan was doing. She said, "She's doing great; her doctor took her off all her meds and her neurologist said they had no reason why they needed to keep seeing her unless something happened. But until then, they decided to release her. But, praise God, she's doing everything a normal child does—running and playing."

When my sister-in-law said they had taken her off her meds and the neurologist had released her, I had to sit down where I was and say, "Thank You, God."

I know God still answers prayer. Like Karen Peck's song says, God likes to work when nothing else will. God's still an on time God.

James R. Harris was born May 30, 1980, to Rick and Betty Harris. He has attended the same church, the Old Mission Church, for twenty-seven years, where his father and late grandfather have both pastored. Today he has started preaching in this church.

A Miracle-Working God

By Donald M. Heard

We live in the fastest growing county in our state. Our little church has grown almost tenfold in the last nine years. We embarked on a building program four years ago and planned a thirty-two thousand square foot multi-purpose building that would seat eight hundred in the sanctuary. Our contract was 2.7 million dollars. Only one bank offered to lend us money, and then only two million. With what we had in the building fund and potential out of pocket costs not covered by the loan, we were 204,000 dollars short of completing the contract price.

The general contractor said the only way we could keep the original contract price was to pay the balance before the expiration date of their offer or the contract would have to be renegotiated and leave several rooms "cold and dark" (no heat, no lights, no ceilings), to be finished at a later time under a second contract. By the time we were able to present the problem to the church, we had ten days left.

The meeting was followed by much prayer, and by the grace of God, we not only reached but exceeded the goal. Our building is expected to be finished in about thirty to forty-five days. We can't praise God enough for all the miracles he has worked in this project.

Donald M. Heard, age fifty-seven, is a resident of Johnston County, North Carolina. He is a deacon, teacher, and member of the building committee at Shiloh Baptist Church.

Isn't God Delighted When He Meets Our Needs?

By Sheryl Hesse

A few years ago, I had lost my job, and we were trying to exist on my unemployment check and what little income my husband was able to bring in as interim pastor of a nearby church.

Just prior to losing my job, we had purchased a small car. We live on an unpaved country lane. The little road had become nothing more than sticky clay mud since it had been raining quite a bit. Suddenly, our car developed a tremendous amount of shaking and wobbling, and we were unable to drive it more than forty-five miles per hour. We took the car to the dealership. After they put the car up on the rack, they just shook their heads and said "We have never seen so much clay mud packed underneath a car...ever!"

We were barely able to buy groceries, let alone pay three hundred dollars to have gravel spread on our road. The only place we knew to go was on our knees. No one knew we had asked God to send us three hundred dollars for gravel.

In a couple of days, a letter came to us in the mail. There was no return address. Inside was a plain sheet of paper. At the top, a single line was typed, "I will supply all your needs according to My riches in glory. God." Tucked in the paper were three one hundred-dollar bills.

A few months later, I awoke one morning to find the corner of my mouth was turning downward. When I tried to smile, only one side of my mouth would turn up. I tried to talk, and funny, garbled words came out, even though I knew clearly in my head what I wanted to say. Drool started oozing out of the side of my mouth.

Since I had lost my job, I had also lost my health insurance and had no money to go to the doctor. Once again, we turned to God in prayer. My husband prayed for me, and then I went to my father's house, where he and my sister lifted me up in prayer. All day long I would cautiously try to smile. Even eating became a problem because the inside of my mouth was numb, and I couldn't tell if I was biting my jaw. I would have to dab the side of my mouth to wipe the saliva away. All day long, my husband and I reminded our heavenly Father that He was our healer.

About 2 a.m. the next morning, I woke up and felt that something was different. I rushed into the bathroom and looked in the mirror, and sure enough, God had given me back my smile! I have had no further problems, praise the Lord! I can only imagine God's delight as He touched the area in my brain that had been touched by a stroke, and as He dropped the three hundred dollars in the mail.

Sheryl Hesse is the office manager at an assisted living community in Winchester, Virginia. She and her husband, Daniel, are also evangelists and missionaries. They live with their three cats, Silver, Gold, and Smoky, and their border collie, Keeland, in their home at the foot of Great North Mountain.

God's Delivering Power

By Jerry Hicks

When I was a teenager I got hooked on drugs, starting with sniffing glue and moving on to harder drugs. In my twenties I ended up hooked on heroin and I did it "mainline." This is where you took the drug through the veins with a needle.

My life was motorcycles and drugs. One day after I had taken drugs, I ended up in an all-night church service. It was at this time the Lord Jesus Christ took hold of my life. I was turned around. That night I was given a blood transfusion. Later, as the Lord worked through my life, I was delivered without going to a rehabilitation center. It was through prayer and letting God take complete control of my life.

Since then I have been blessed to record many CDs of praise to my precious Lord. He has allowed me to do things and go to places I otherwise would have only dreamed of. His wonderful power in my life is my sustaining source, and it all came from prayer. My mother and wife are the two largest influences in my walk with God. They never gave up on me.

To sum it up, I guess you could say prayer took me from a road leading to nowhere to a place of peace and contempt. I know prayer is the key to what the Lord Jesus had done in my life.

Jerry Hicks is the president of Eye on the Prize Ministries. He has been married for thirty-nine years and has four children and eight grandchildren.

God Truly Blessed Me

By Karen Hinton

On November 12, 2006, I awoke with a boil located in my groin area. I put a hot compress on it to get it to drain, and by Wednesday I was trying to contact my primary care physician to get an antibiotic. At 8:15 a.m. on November 16, my sister Margie called to see if I had heard back. I told her I was going to take my granddaughters to school and then I was going to the ER because I hadn't heard from him.

My "miracles" started from that point on. I remember nothing about the drive to the school or the ER, and I remember nothing about the next week. My sister called my cell phone at about 2:30 that afternoon, and a nurse in the ER answered it, telling her they were admitting me to the ICU and I was still very ill. My blood pressure was 60/40 when I got there, and I was in septic shock. I was dying. It was 7:30 p.m. before they were able to operate. I had nectrozing faciitus, better known as "flesh-eating bacteria."

During the next three days, I had four surgeries. One was to remove a football-sized area of damaged tissue. The others were for more debridement and clean up, and to remove a four-inch blood cot in the wound. My family was called in to see me one last time if they wanted. At first, the doctor thought she would have to amputate the leg from the hip down, and then they were concerned it would "eat" through the femoral artery. If I made it through the night, it would be a "miracle." My family was told I would be in recovery from this for many months. I was going to need a long-term continuous care facility.

After one week at Stillwater, I was life-flighted to Tulsa. I had congestive heart failure from all the fluids they had pumped into me to get my blood pressure up. I was at that hospital for one week, and then I went to the long-term facility. I was equipped with a machine called a "wound vac," which was hooked on my wound, and then I was sent home on December 23, 2006.

I was told conflicting information about my annual and sick pay from work and my hospital insurance. I was required to have home healthcare three times a week. So, needless to say, the stress and worry about all that sent me into major depression. However, God did not just stop with healing my body; He made it possible for me to return to work just when I had used up all of my sick and annual days. My insurance also ended because I would no longer be considered an employee.

God truly blessed me. I tell everyone who asks how I am how God healed me. God was not through with me yet, and I give Him all the praise and glory. I might be having reconstructive surgery in October or November. The plastic surgeon asked if I had plans in August, and I told him yes. The first and third weeks of August, I will be going to the gospel singing in Lebanon, Missouri, and at Seminole, Oklahoma. He said, "I will see you again August 31, 2007." Keep me in your prayers.

Karen Hinton is a 57-year-old woman and has lived and worked in Stillwater, Oklahoma, for ten years. She works as a substance abuse counselor/drug court coordinator for the Payne County Drug Court.

Guardian Angel

By Jack Richard Hodge

My wife Linda and I decided we needed to get away for the day. Away from all the stress we were having in our life. I called Park Vista to check the Sunday menu for the day. The breakfast buffet was served from 6:30 a.m. to 12 noon. We decided to take our time and go for lunch.

Lunch was fantastic. We started with the baked French onion soup and we split a roast beef sandwich with fries—excellent choice. Then came dessert, chocolate raspberry dream. There was Coffee to drink. All was fabulous. As we ate, we were looking down over Gatlinburg. What a fabulous view of the city from high on the mountain. Our waitress, Anne McNeeley, was fantastic. Anne's Husband Jon was one of the chefs on duty, as was Jose Perez. This was a very relaxing lunch. We were glad we picked Park Vista for our day of relaxation.

We came down off the mountain from Park Vista. It was a very steep driveway! As we turned off Airport Road, I realized I had no breaks. The town was very busy, and the sidewalks were loaded with people. Both lanes of traffic were extremely busy. I pulled down into first gear to slow me down, frantically pumping the breaks as hard as I could. I was not slowing down! I tried running into the curb to slow me down, but with no luck.

A young man started to step off the curb into the street. I laid on my horn as Linda frantically waved him back. All of a sudden, there was a police officer and a wrecker in front of me, removing an illegally parked limousine. I almost hit the police officer, missing him by only inches. We waved and yelled, "We can't stop!" to the officer. Although startled by his own near miss, he called to another officer in a vehicle to tell him our vehicle had no brakes and to try to use his vehicle to stop us before we hit someone.

I had just enough time to swing into the other lane around the wrecker and back into my lane without being hit or hitting anyone. I was praying all the time. It looked as if we would have to hit a light pole to stop this rampage.

Then I heard a siren. The police Jeep pulled in front of me and braked to stop my van. At this time, my guardian angel really took control. The brakes worked long enough for me to stop me before I ran into the back of the Jeep and held until I put the van in park and then the brake pedal returned to the floor. At this moment I was thanking my Lord Jesus for my guardian angel.

Officer Matt Smith was the officer in the vehicle. I cannot thank him enough for his kindness and help, and for being so understanding.

Sergeant Chuck Reagan was the officer I almost hit. I do apologize to him. Gatlinburg can be proud of the men on their force; I am. My wife Linda and I could have been killed or killed someone. But our guardian angel was there to protect us. What was to be a stress-free day showed us what real stress was.

Jack Hodge is the author of Poems from the Spirit, *the CEO and founder of "The Jack Hodge Gospel Show," a gospel singer, and a songwriter. He writes a column called "Jack's Corner."*

A Love Offering

By Nella Jenkins

Several years ago, we were on our way to Canada to sing on the Indian reservation. We stopped in St. Louis, Missouri to eat. After we finished, we came back outside only to find our van, trailer, and more than ten thousand dollars worth of products and equipment were stolen. We had no insurance on the trailer. The rig was recovered the next day, and the trailer was empty.

All of our phone calls—to and from Canada, to and from the insurance company, and to and from our prayer warriors—totaled $700.01. During our tour we went without sound equipment, but around forty souls prayed for us in the altars. When we returned from our tour we also found we didn't have the funds to pay the phone bill. We took it to the Lord in prayer and tried not to worry. My sister and I were old maids, so we had a tendency to worry a lot!

The last day before it got cut off, we went to the P.O. box and there was the sweetest card from Karen Peck. She had heard about our disaster and sent us a love offering. Can you guess how much it was? Yes. Seven hundred dollars. I guess God figured we could come up with the penny!

Nella Jenkins, from Texas, travels full-time with Jenkins and Company and sings in places no other groups will go.

God Is Our Everything

By Patty Johnson

It was December of 2003. I was depressed because I was no longer able to work due to back problems. My blood pressure was 220/198. I was preparing for Christmas. On December 20, my father-in-law passed away peacefully in his sleep. My mother-in-law's mother passed away unexpectedly on December 31st from cancer. On January 1, 2004, my uncle passed away.

On February 24, 2004, I had a heart cath to check for blockage which might be causing my high blood pressure. I did fine. While waiting the six hours to be released, my husband David "coded" right there in the hospital. The doctor who had just checked my films was going off duty, but he responded to the code blue. Through May, David had five stents put in.

In June 2004, my mother was diagnosed with cancer. She had surgery, and a colostomy bag was necessary. In September 2004, David had to have a defibrillator implanted. God never left us. Mom wanted her surgery reversed before Christmas. It was a success, but she still had her cancer. We began chemo treatments in March 2005. They were not successful. We, her two daughters and three sons, cared for her in a coma state at home for a week. We were there when she stopped breathing at 3 a.m. on June 13, 2005. She had endured to the end and was at last with God.

David wasn't well during this time, but he knew I wanted to be with Mom. Now we had to see to his problems. On June 27, 2005, an echocardiogram showed a massive vegetation on the wires of the defibrillator inside his heart. Open heart surgery was the only way to remove the wires and the vegetation. It proved to be a staph infection which had also spread to his lungs. He was in the hospital for thirteen days and was home with an antibiotic IV for six weeks. I was trained to change the IV bags, and home nursing checked on us once a week.

God was with us every second. We were able to travel to The Breaks, Virginia, for the annual gospel sing. Praise the Lord; He's my everything. We are preparing now to have a defibrillator put back in. David's heart is working at only thirty-five percent. God's our everything, and everything will be okay. "If God is for us, who can be against us?" (Romans 8:31).

Patty Johnson lives in rural southern Ohio. A lifelong farmer, she has been married to her husband David for forty-two years now. They have a daughter, two sons, and four grandchildren.

The Tithe

By Helen Jones

During the early seventies, I was a church pianist. I volunteered my playing at Sunday school for a Methodist church and would drive about five minutes to a Nazarene church for Sunday morning worship service.

One Sunday the Nazarene minister gave the congregation an alert about the financial situation of the church. They were about to lose their beautiful church building. When they had moved to the suburbs, all the members didn't go with them and there was now a new building with a financial burden.

At the time, I did not tithe yet. I knew I should. That Sunday, however, I had a fifty-dollar bill in my purse, and I slipped it into the minister's hand as I left. I told him to use it wherever he needed it.

Six days later, a local recording studio called me and told me they had heard I played gospel music. I was asked to go to the studio and audition. I went up that afternoon and auditioned for a gospel group's recording. I got the job! The next afternoon (Sunday) we started recording. My pay was sixty dollars—fifty dollars back that I had given the minister plus ten dollars.

God is so good, and I praise Him for teaching me to tithe and always trusting in Him!

Helen Jones is a gospel pianist, music director, and author. She is originally from Cleveland, Tennessee. She resides in Charlotte, North Carolina, where she instructs forty weekly piano students. She has been teaching since the age of twelve! She has also written Looking at Chords, *a common-sense method for playing the piano.*

Closet Cleaning

By Dino Kartsonakis

I could write a book on the miracles Cheryl and I have experienced throughout the years in our ministry. But to be current, Cheryl has a praise report for women who are thinking about cleaning out their closets. Cheryl says, "You can never give without God noticing and giving more back to you!"

Just recently, Cheryl and I were in Moscow with the Rick Renner Ministries, and God laid it upon Cheryl's heart to give some of her beautiful designer clothes to women in need in Russia who she ministered to while she was there.

In preparing to televise our weekly show at Trinity Broadcasting Network, Cheryl went shopping at the Grand Glitz clothing store at the Branson Landing in Branson, Missouri, and selected fifteen beautiful outfits to wear for the series. After selecting all of these clothes, the owner of the shop took us aside and said she would like for Cheryl to have as a gift the whole wardrobe to wear on television and concert engagements—you just can't out-give God.

So ladies, clean out those closets and give! Now expect God's multiplied blessings.

Dino Kartsonakis, America's Piano Showman, presents a dynamic show in Branson, Missouri. He has headlined at Carnegie Hall, and will soon perform at Lincoln Center in New York City. Dino has received a Grammy nomination for Chariots of Fire *as well as a Grammy acknowledgement for* The Apostle *soundtrack, and eight Gospel Music Association Dove Awards.*

Hannah calls me Daddy

By Eric Kaunitz

My wife was a divorced single mom when we met. My wife and her ex-hubby both decided that, in the best interest of their son, Levi, they would not quarrel over him and would be kind to each other. As part of their agreement, Ray promised her he would not let Levi call another woman "Mommy," and my wife agreed she would not let Levi call another man "Daddy," an agreement I strongly support! Ray is a good daddy to Levi.

As Levi and I bonded, he wanted to call me a daddy-like name. So he came up with "Pop." He was three years old at the time. During the wedding, we had a family dedication time, during which Levi came to the altar with us. I promised him I would love him as my own child and be a father to him. Levi is glad he has two daddies.

On July 12, 2006, my wife and I had a child of our own named Hannah. We felt it was important that Hannah call me "Pop" instead of "Daddy," so Levi would not feel like he was different and not part of the family. But I must confess to you this was a source of pain for me. I think the desire to be called "Daddy" is built in every man, but this was a sacrifice I was willing to make for Levi's sake.

The most amazing thing happened in May of this year! I took the family to Dallas for a weekend trip. We had a blast! We went to Six Flags Over Texas and the Fort Worth Zoo. Levi, now six and a half, could ride a lot of the "big boy" rides. On the way back home, we stopped at a Burger King drive-through to get a bite to eat. I parked in the parking lot so we could eat and so my wife could nurse Hannah in private.

I was in the driver's seat, Levi was beside me in the front passenger's seat, and Hannah was sitting in my wife's lap in the back seat directly behind Levi. After Hannah was done "eating," she stood up on her mommy's lap and started tapping Levi on the back of his head and saying "Da, Da, Da, Da," which was just a random sound she made. My wife said, "Levi, Hannah is trying to get your attention."

Levi responded by saying, "No Mommy, I think she is talking to Pop."

My wife said, "Why do you say that?"

Levi said, "She's saying 'Da, Da, Da, Da.' After all, he is her Daddy and I think she should call him 'Daddy.'"

My wife and I look at each other with amazement! I tried to explain to Levi, "We want Hannah to call me 'Pop' so you don't feel like I don't love you as much."

These were Levi's exact words: "Well Pop, here's the deal. I have a daddy and you are her daddy, so I think she should call you 'Daddy.' Besides, I think of you as my real daddy anyway."

Tears start shooting from my eyes. I said, "Levi, that is the nicest thing anyone has ever said to me!"

Levi said, "Thank you, Pop. But I want Hannah to call you 'Daddy.'"

So God used a six-year-old boy to bring me such joy and to relieve a source of pain for me. And by the way, Hannah now calls me "Daddy."

Eric Kaunitz is a 33-year-old computer/network technician from Gilmer, Texas.

God's Healing Touch

By Mark King

My dad had been having mini strokes for several months when his neurologist suggested he have a CT scan to see what was going on. My dad being the joker he is, said, "Go ahead; it's pretty much empty up there anyway!"

The CT scan showed very small bleeds but nothing to be exceptionally worried about. What did concern them more was that his carotid artery was ninety-either percent blocked and would require surgery to open it. The surgery was scheduled for the next morning.

They were able to clean the artery but in the process, his hypoglossal verve was damaged. This is the nerve that affects swallowing. He wound up staying in the hospital for two weeks trying to see if they could get him to swallow, to no avail.

It was at this point the doctors were talking about putting a feeding tube in so he could receive much-needed nourishment. The night before the surgery, my wife and I went to see him. He was getting ready to go have another x-ray of the carotid arteries, so before he went downstairs, I told him we needed to pray. I can't explain it, but a calm came over me as I prayed. The words just flowed as we prayed for God's divine intervention.

He went down for the x-ray and came back about an hour later. Upon his return, he said, "I think I swallowed a little while I was on the x-ray table." Tears were welling up in my eyes, as I knew he had experienced a mighty touch from the Lord. We immediately called the nurse, who then called the doctor. They postponed the surgery until they did a swallowing test the next morning.

The test went very well and he was starting to swallow. The surgery was cancelled! No feeding tube was needed!

God is good all the time, and all the time God is good!

Mark King resides in Salem, Virginia, with his wife of twenty-two years, Jody. They have a set of twenty-year-old twins, Tim and Courtney.

Lakeland's Singing Church

By Charles Kirby

We are celebrating ten years of "Saturday Nights in Lakeland" at Lake Gibson Nazarene Church on January 5, 2008. It all began on the first Saturday night in January of 1998. A packed church experienced an exciting evening of southern gospel music. It was the inspiration of that night that motivated us to begin the "Saturday Night in Lakeland" concert series.

Since that inaugural event, we have been bringing to Lakeland the biggest names in southern gospel music. These groups appear in concert every Saturday night from January through the middle of April. New seasons begin in September with an abbreviated schedule through December.

Since we started "Saturday Nights in Lakeland," it has transformed our church. We have had a growth explosion in membership, attendance, and finance. Worship attendance has increased from an average of 140 to 1,322. Hundreds of people have made spiritual decisions for Christ during this period. We have had to enlarge our worship center, platform, and choir area to accommodate the crowds and growth.

Since "Saturday Nights in Lakeland" have been so successful, we began "Sunday Nights in Lakeland" in 2005. This has allowed us to give people the opportunity to see more southern gospel groups than we have room for on Saturday nights. When many churches across America have stopped having church on Sunday nights, we are proving Sunday nights are not dead in Lakeland, Florida, at Lake Gibson Nazarene Church!

As a kid growing up in Jackson, Tennessee, I became a fan of southern gospel music through the Blackwood Brothers, Statesmen Quartet, and Speer Family. Through the years my pastoral ministry has reaped wonderful results by using southern gospel groups in my churches. It has been a thrill and a joy to be the host of southern gospel groups coming to Lakeland for our concert series. As a result, we are now known as Lakeland's singing church. I praise God for the wonderful opportunities He is giving us to keep southern gospel music alive in our Central Florida area!

Charles Kirby is the senior pastor of Lake Gibson Nazarene Church in Lakeland, Florida. He assumed the pastorate on November 15, 1998. He preaches in conferences across America and Canada. He has pastored churches from California to Virginia, Texas, Florida, and Indiana.

Just One More Miracle

By Tom and Linda Kline

On one of our CD's by the Dove Brothers, they sing the song "One More Miracle." This has become one of our favorite songs over the past year.

As we traveled to Arizona this past winter, we encountered several minor problems with our motor home and our towed vehicle. Each time our problem was taken care of and we were back in our SUV (which was being towed) listening to our CDs, it seems the Dove Brothers would come on singing "One More Miracle." This song has come to mean so much to us.

In June, we were facing another difficult time when we needed "just one more miracle." After some testing and an MRI, they found a tumor on my spine. Needless to say, my husband and I were both a bit upset not knowing the outcome. As we traveled about ninety miles to visit with the neurosurgeon, once again we were blessed by the song "One More Miracle."

A few days later, I needed to go for a brain scan and was going to meet my husband at the hospital. As I was alone on my way to the hospital, once again I heard "One More Miracle" and broke down and cried, just praying to God there was one more miracle for me.

Now, a month later, the surgery is past. It was very successful with no paralyses, the tumor was benign, and I am getting back my strength. God is so good to us, and what a blessing it is to have those who can sing so those of us who don't sing can be blessed by this great music.

We will be looking for the Dove Brothers at NQC to personally thank them for such a great song.

Tom and Linda Kline were raised in Christian homes, attended the same church, and were eventually married in the same church. They have a son and daughter who are both married.

A Normal Day

By Lori Klinger

October 29, 2003, was a normal day at the Klinger house. Lee and I took Kevin to school and did some errands. I then returned to the school to tie up some loose ends on a fundraiser I was setting up. As I stood in the school office, I felt a snap toward the back of my head. Thinking it was one of the students teasing me, I didn't pay any attention until I got very sick in my stomach and began to feel a pounding headache. I drove home with God's help. I could not remember how I got there even though we only lived four miles away. As I got into the house, I collapsed onto the floor, screaming. Lee came over and got me to the couch. He called our chiropractor since I had never had anything happen like this before, he told me to get to the ER immediately. After a few tests, I was told I had a leaking brain aneurysm and would need surgery to repair it.

I was told I could have a stroke or even die before or during surgery. I had very low blood pressure, so they could not operate until the next day. As I lay in bed that night after my family had gone to sleep, I had this incredible peace in my heart. I was scared to death but I knew that if I didn't wake up here, I would be with my Lord Jesus in heaven. I asked my family before they went to the waiting room to sleep that if God chose to take me home, would they be in heaven someday with me? They assured me they would, and I was able to rest with that assurance. Pastor Mowen and Pastor Randy were both there by 5:00 a.m. to have prayer with my family and me. I was already on dozens of prayer chains all around the world. I was in the hands of the Great Physician.

I awoke in the recovery room after eight hours of brain surgery. One of our pastor's wives was my nurse. It was a blessing indeed to have a familiar face with me in the recovery room. The surgeon came to see me and told me everything went very well, and that I might have some memory loss as well as some other "hindrances," but therapy would take care of most of it.

As I lay in that hospital bed for the next few days, I could not help but thank God for the miracle of allowing me to live through a brain aneurysm rupture. Not many folks get a second chance like that.

The physical therapists were sent in to do evaluations. After they finished, I was told I needed no therapy! I was discharged from the hospital seven days after surgery. I was told I would need medication for a while, but not long-term! The meds I needed were three thousand dollars for three weeks. Because we had not yet switched insurance companies, my medication cost fifty dollars and the hospital bill was covered in full!

I was released to return to work twelve weeks after surgery with no limitations! I have had no major side effects from the surgery, unless you count my testimony as a side effect! Brian Free and Assurance sings "I have been healed!" and I love to share my story with people so they, too, may come to know my Jesus!

Lori Klinger is forty-three years old and has been married to her high school sweetheart, Lee, for twenty years. She is the mother of Kevin. The family lives in Northumberland, Pennsylvania and attends Crossroads Nazarene Church, where Klinger is actively involved in several ministries.

The Lord Lifted My Addiction

By Joe Lanier

I smoked cigarettes for years and years, and was severely addicted to nicotine. In fact, I'd smoke a chain if I could light it. My health was in question and I had a literally constant hacking cough. I needed to quit smoking. I tried the patches, but they didn't work.

I finally gave up on my own willpower and went to a church in Fort Worth, Texas. This church had a reputation for assisting people with addictions. I went down to the pulpit area after the Wednesday evening service, where the pastor and some of the church deacons laid hands on me and prayed that the Lord would lift my addiction. He did, and I haven't had a cigarette since—and that was seventeen years ago. Were there incidences where I somewhat desired a smoke? Yes, but the "had to have" desire was and still is totally gone. Thank You, Jesus!

Joe Lanier is a senior citizen from Texas who is now semi-retired from the security equipment industry. He assists his local church with volunteer audio and video duties, including a tape outreach ministry. I also helps with monthly financial support for several international ministries.

Our Miracle

By Brian and Monique Linton

My wife and I have been married for twelve years. We, like everyone else, dreamed of having a family. After two miscarriages, we finally started going to the doctor to find out what the problem was. That was when we heard the news no one likes to hear: "You will never be able to have children."

We had tons of pastors prophesy that God would bless us with a child one day, and after eleven years of hearing this, my faith began to waver. It seemed I could trust God for everything else, but I did not have the faith to believe He could bless us with a child. Well, as I write this we are going to be adopting a newborn. The mother is due any day. This is a private adoption, and only God could have opened the door!

Brian and Monique Linton have a music ministry, and have been traveling and sharing God's love through words and song. They are the music minister and children's minister of their home church, North Pointe Tabernacle.

The Instant Answer

By Shanna Locker

I have worked as a booking agent for Liberty Quartet in Boise, Idaho, for almost a decade. It was so much more than just a job; it was a ministry in and of itself. The relationships formed over the years with the people I worked with have been the most rewarding ones I've ever experienced.

After about eight years I started to feel restless, like it was maybe time to give it up and look for something else to do. I prayed for many months, seeking God and His guidance before I did anything. Silence was my only answer.

One day in October the phone rang, and it was the most amazing job offer out of the blue with Dell. The man in charge of the business attended the church my dad pastored, and for reasons unknown to me, he called. His words were, "I just found out I must hire one more person by tomorrow morning. Would you be able to come in at 3:00 p.m. for an interview."

It was 12:30 p.m. then. Not wanting to just throw away an opportunity that might have been heaven sent, I said, "Sure, I'll be there."

I began praying harder than ever before, seeking what God wanted for me. I was in the car a couple of hours later heading to the interview. I stopped at the stop sign at the end of my road. My exact words to God were, "Dear Lord, if You want me to continue working for Liberty, You're going to have to make it as plain as if it were a billboard in front of my face."

Just then, while I was in mid-sentence, a white cab over a Peterbuilt semi truck pulled up right beside me. It was pulling a flatbed trailer with a large box strapped to it. The box was very dirty and someone had written in the dirt with their finger. There, in huge capital letters diagonally across the box, was the word "liberty."

I looked up, more than amazed, and said, "Well, God, that was fast. Tell me why I'm going to this interview?" I pulled out my camera phone and followed the truck until I could safely take a photo of the box, because I knew no one would believe me when I told them about this.

I went to the interview, and when they asked me why I wanted to work there, I told them my story. They just shook their heads and said nothing, but what an opportunity it was to speak to them about God and how He works.

I called my boss with the quartet and told him this story. His exact words were, "Well, all I can say is bad for Dell, good for Liberty."

People all over this country and Canada have heard my story of an instant answer to prayer and are as amazed by it as I still am. God can even use a semi truck hauling a dirty box for His purposes, and I'm so thankful for how He works!

Shanna Locker has been married for twenty-three years to her husband, George, and has two children. She has worked as a booking agent the last ten years for a southern gospel quartet from Boise, Idaho.

Memories of George

By Shanna Locker

March 17, 2005. For me it is a date I'll never forget. I was shopping for groceries and my phone rang. It was my husband, and his exact words were, "Honey, George Younce just called for you."

Knowing my husband's joking nature, I said, "Yeah right. Good one, Bill."

His reply was, "I'm serious. He called and left his cell number and wants you to call him back."

I took just what I had in my cart to the checkout and went directly home. I called, and there was George's weak but sweet voice. I told him, "Hi George, this is Shanna with Liberty Quartet. My husband told me you called and wanted to talk with me."

He said, "A friend of mine from The Couriers gave me a copy of *Liberty's Live in Alaska* DVD and I wanted to tell you what I thought about it."

Here are a few quotes from that conversation: "What a wonderful bass singer ya'll have. Tell him for me I'm gonna kill him! Nobody is allowed to sing better than me!" He said, "I love the presentation, don't change a thing. Just change your songs now and then." He also said, "I love the blend and smooth harmonies, what a great video."

To sum it up, during his last days while lying in bed, too weak to hold his own phone, he called to encourage another quartet and in doing so showed me just who George really was. I told him how honored I was to hear from him and how, from early childhood, I had loved his music. My dad would wake us up with some gospel groups' music—usually The Cathedrals or The Kingsmen—almost every morning. The call lasted about five minutes, but the memory of the call will last forever!

Twenty-seven days later George went to see the Lord. What an awesome man! I told Ernie Haase this story in November 2005 at a Signature Sound concert in Nampa, Idaho, and he listened with tears flowing.

Shanna Locker has been married for twenty-three years to her husband, George, and has two children. She has worked as a booking agent the last ten years for a southern gospel quartet from Boise, Idaho.

Listening to God's Spirit

By Jerry Malone

The year was 1970, and I had received a call from The Coachmen singing group in Memphis, Tennessee. They were searching for a pianist for their trio, and my name had been passed on to them. I had studied piano for ten years and taught it full-time with about seventy students weekly, and I had about five years of quartet experience as pianist.

My wife and I made the trip from St. Louis down to Memphis and met with a great bunch of guys, rehearsed with them, and visited in their homes. Much discussion was held, and we felt the tug of the Lord that this might be His will. We told them we'd pray about this and get back with them. We then discussed this with my pastor who had been my pastor since my boyhood. He was not too favorable about this decision of leaving the church. Of course, he was looking at losing a pianist for church and there was a little bit of selfishness on his part—this he would tell me later.

My dream was seemingly shot down, and I called the group and told them I was not sure and that my pastor was a little negative about my leaving. I told them they'd better keep looking for another pianist. When I hung up, there was no relief like when a burden has been lifted, but rather a heaviness. I pondered this decision over the next week, and my wife and I both felt we had missed God on this one. I was going to have to go against my pastor's viewpoint on the matter.

I called the group back up and asked if they had filled the position yet. They had not, and I told them we were coming. Moving arrangements were made, our house went on the market for sale, and the ball was set into motion. A sigh of relief filled my wife and me, as we knew we had obeyed God on this opportunity.

About a week later, I received a telephone call from my pastor. He very humbly told me he thought he had missed God in convincing me to not move away. He said he did this out of selfishness and said he was very sorry for his input. I told him that after much prayer, I had gone ahead and called the group back to tell them we were coming, and that we had made arrangements for the transition even though my pastor felt otherwise.

Through this, I have learned that our pastors are godly men and I value and appreciate their input, but sometimes we have to launch out on our own when God speaks. Sometimes there is an opportunity for us even though it may go against those who stand over us and feel differently.

After several years of traveling with The Coachmen, I went back into my career of teaching piano and furthered my education by studying piano tuning and rebuilding. We have lived in Kalamazoo, Michigan, from 1984 to the present. After almost thirty-five years of building a piano tuning business here with some twelve hundred clients, I had begun to hear the voice of the Spirit that a change was coming. Due to a chronic pain condition in my body, I had to give up the business, and God provided a buyer for the business. So I am in retirement and waiting on God for the next stage of my life. Who knows? I may end up as pianist for a southern gospel group again in the near future.

Jerry Malone lives with his wife Jerri in Southwest Michigan. They have two daughters, two sons-in-law, and four grandchildren.

A Small Miracle

By Sharon Manprin

Jesus does talk to us. It was a hot summer morning and I had to go into town for some supplies for my job. The paint had started to peel off my car about six months prior, and I had put off stopping by the dealership. In my rush that morning, I had all the windows down, and all of a sudden I heard nothing. It was like the first snow—so quiet.

I heard this voice say, "Stop now" I thought, *What?* Was I speeding? I looked around for a police car. There was no one but rushing cars going by. Then the noise from the outside started again. I went another half a mile and the same thing happened. Again, there was total silence, and the voice said, "Stop now." I looked up as I was going by the car dealership, and I said out loud, "Okay."

I went inside and told the man about my paint. He came out to check the numbers on my car, and it turns out that day was the last day for recall. I got a free paint job and said thank you to Jesus for the silly small things. Jesus had His watchful eye on me. It was something so small, but such a miracle.

Sharon Manprin works as an Alzheimer's coordinator at Golden Umbrella in Redding, California. She has been married to her husband Ron for twenty-five years. They have five grown children and eight grandsons.

Angel Unawares

By Glenda Mayberry

Nearly ten years ago, while the world was mourning the loss of Princess Diana, our family had its own tragedy. On August 28, 1997, my daughter was coming to visit. It was shortly after dark. Carrying our nine-month-old grandson down a declining sidewalk, she tripped over the family black lab and fell on the concrete sidewalk. Stephen Wayne had been seriously injured with a fractured skull. The next few days were filled with tests and waiting for the swelling to subside. There were lots of family and friends who supported us with prayer and were filled with concern.

On Sunday morning the doctors came to the conclusion that emergency surgery might be needed to find out why Stephen Wayne's blood count was so low; blood was being lost somewhere. There was some bleeding in the brain, but how much? Immediately, my daughter called home and asked everyone to pray; they were going to test one more time before going to surgery.

She was watching TBN with Rod Parsley, whose guest was The Martins. While preaching, Rod Parsley stopped in the middle of his sermon and looked right in the camera and said, "That baby is healed!" Jonathon had just found that his child was ill and Rod was referring to his baby, but at the time my daughter took it as God's Word. The blood test it came back at a high enough count, so surgery was not necessary yet.

While in the hospital, the nurses quickly discovered if they sang "Jesus Loves Me," Stephen Wayne would quickly calm down. They had seen the family do this, so they followed suit.

After several months, the fracture was separating instead of closing up. It was decided to send Stephen Wayne to St. Louis Cardinal Glennon Hospital. God knows even the smallest details and supplies we need. After the surgery, we were told Stephen Wayne would need to wear a helmet for several months to protect his head. After several phone calls, my daughter discovered these helmets were very expensive. Finally, someone directed her back to a gentleman at the Cardinal Glennon hospital who had an office in the basement. We made an appointment and set off to get Stephen Wayne's head measured and have the helmet made. When we went to pick up the helmet, my daughter asked how much we owed him and was prepared to pay several hundred dollars. He said, "Thirteen dollars." We looked at him in disbelief, and he said, "That is correct." This was a miracle, as we knew what these helmets usually cost.

Several months later we were going to bring this gentleman a thank you card while we were at the hospital getting Stephen Wayne's stitches out. We got on the elevator and took it down to the basement, but there was nothing there. We went back up and asked the receptionist at the desk if he had moved. She looked at us and told us she didn't know anything about an office in the basement. No one had a clue what we were talking about. We were there not once but twice, and we spoke with this man. We fully believe he was an angel, unaware to us.

Months later, Stephen Wayne, whom we were told would have to relearn all his motor skills, memorized the entire "Light up the Night" soundtrack by The New Hinsons. He is now almost eleven years old, has been tested, and scored with the mental capacity of a 16.9-year-old. He has also spent his recess at school sharing Sunday school lessons with a classmate who never attended church. A miracle!

Glenda Mayberry resides in Jonesboro, Illinois. She has been married to Wayne Mayberry for thirty-one years and has two children, Carrie and Travis, and five grandchildren. She has been employed at the Southeast Missourian *newspaper for fifteen years as the account executive for the real estate market for print and Internet.*

Raising from the Dead

By Elaine McCauslin

One October day in 2005, I received a call from my dad saying my mom was in the hospital. She had, what they thought, was a seizure, and the doctors were running tests. Nothing could be determined, so the doctors put her on seizure medicine and sent her home. We began praying that God would heal her of these problems.

Over the course of the next couple of months, my mom had what they thought were two more seizures. Finally, in January of 2006, my mom was home and began having, what my dad thought, was a seizure. My dad called 911, and she was taken to the hospital. Our family was not convinced these were just seizures, so we asked the doctors to run more tests, all the while praying God would touch her. Living twelve hundred miles away did not make things easy for me. Trying to determine when to fly home was agonizing.

It was determined that my mom had an irregular heartbeat and would need surgery on her heart. Again, we prayed. I quickly booked a flight home for the next morning so that I could be there for her surgery. The next morning, while on my way to the airport, I received a call saying my mom's heart had stopped beating during the night. As you can expect, it felt like I could not get to my mom fast enough.

I prayed the whole flight. After arriving and seeing that the situation was under control, I began talking with the doctors and nurses about what had happened. They told me my mom had stopped breathing and her heart had stopped beating for more than three minutes. They indicated that usually they cannot bring someone back after that length of time. The one nurse said, "Your mom died, but now she is alive."

I then began to explain that it was God who touched her because we were praying.

God works in mysterious ways, but I know when you pray and give things completely over to God, His perfect plan will be accomplished. Sometimes, as with my mom, He heals. Other times, He allows situations to happen but will always give us the strength to go through them. That's why they are called valleys.

Elaine McCauslin resides in Biglerville, Pennsylvania. She grew up in Tampa, Florida, and traveled with her family's southern gospel group, The Laceys, until she got married in 1997. She currently works as an assistant to the president of Gettysburg College.

A Miracle of Healing

By Carolyn F. McCoy

Yes, God is real! Since the beginning of January 2007, I have had many rough days due to back problems. I recall one particular January morning, prior to my surgery, in which God let me know He was real.

Early on this morning I awakened in terrible pain. I prayed and asked God to help me bear the pain. I glanced at the clock beside my bed, and the time was 4:13 a.m. I said, "God, why 4:13 a.m. in the morning?" Immediately my mind went to Philippians 4:13, which says "I can do all things through Christ who strengthens me."

That was God's way of answering my prayer that morning. That was His way of assuring me He was going to be right there with me through the surgery and all that it entailed. Little did I know I would need that verse countless times in the coming days.

When dismissed from the hospital, I could not walk without the aid of a walker. I saw God perform a miracle in my life as He enabled me to go from a walker, to a cane, to nothing.

Jesus Christ is real and He is still performing miracles today. How do I know that? I was the recipient of a miracle. All Christians are recipients of the miracle of salvation, which is the greatest miracle of all time. I thank God that someone told me about Christ and allowed me to experience that miracle of His healing my soul. I also thank Him for the miracle of healing in my body. Yes, God is real! To Him be all the praise and glory for what He has done in my life!

Carolyn F. McCoy resides near Honea Path, South Carolina. She and her husband Leonard have been married for twenty-nine years and have one son, Terry. They are active members of Mount Bethel Baptist Church in Belton.

A Manifestation of God's Love

By Joseph McCray

"God is our refuge and strength, a very present help in time of need" (Psalm 46:1).

On October 19, 2005, I decided I wanted to go hiking at Catoctin Mountains or biking on the NCR trail, both in Maryland. I was getting a late start, so I chose biking. I drove to Monkton to begin my bicycle ride to New Freedom, Pennsylvania, and back, approximately twenty-nine miles. When I reached New Freedom, I turned back.

After some time my wife, Lillian, got concerned that I had not returned home or called. She called my cell phone number. A policeman answered her call. She identified herself as my wife. The policeman informed her that I had collapsed on the trail and was presently at St. Joseph's Hospital in Baltimore. I was approximately one-quarter of a mile from the end of my trip when I had a sudden cardiac arrest. I lay there for possibly a few minutes before my seemingly lifeless body was discovered by someone on the trail. He summoned help from three women (Cappy, Kathy, and Joy) who were riding by on their bikes. God set His plan into motion. Two of the women who had CPR training many years ago immediately started to perform CPR. The third woman dialed 911 and directed the ambulance to me when it arrived. The EMS personnel performed initial life-saving techniques and drove me to the nearest heart hospital, St. Joseph's.

When entering the hospital, my chances of surviving were slim. I was completely non responsive. To protect my brain and heart, my body temperature was lowered to about eighty-nine degrees Fahrenheit for about twenty-hour hours. I had two more cardiac arrests a week after entering the hospital. Besides heart complications, I had various infections, pulmonary problems, pneumonia, etc. It was determined that a quadruple bypass was necessary. In addition, a defibrillator implantation was necessary to reduce the risk of future cardiac ventricular fibrillation. On November 25, I went home to continue the recovery process. After various tribulations, I miraculously recovered.

The only reason I am alive to write this is because of God's infinite grace. Upon meditating on my experience, several facts entered my mind. If I had gone hiking at Catoctin Mountains, I would have had the sudden cardiac arrest in an isolated area where I would not be discovered for an indefinite period of time. I don't know the time between the discovery of my body and CPR, but that time interval was critical in preventing major disabilities. It was not a coincidence that Cappy, Kathy, and Joy, all of whom had some CPR experience and were concerned about trying to save a life, "just happened" to be riding by. It was part of God's plan to rescue me. They had not planned to ride that section of the trail that day and then suddenly decided to do so. The incident also occurred near St. Joseph's Hospital, which is one of the top cardiac hospitals in the nation.

This was one of the best and worst experiences of my life. It was a blessing in that God again demonstrated the magnitude of His love, faithfulness, and power, even though I was not worthy. It is really awesome in that every step in my recovery had to be perfectly orchestrated to insure my survival, and only God could perform that miracle. The whole experience gave me further insight into God's goodness and love for His children and makes me realize that every day that we live is indeed a great blessing. Praise the Lord! I am so grateful.

Joseph McCray was born in New Jersey in April 1935. He has bachelors and masters degrees in electronic engineering. His employment was with the Department of Defense; he retired in 1998. He and his wife live in Pennsylvania near their two daughters. McCray's primary interests are Christianity and outdoor activities.

Seeking the Truth

By Mario McDonald

I was born and raised in Cuba. During my years in high school and later in college, my teachers always scared me about the "afterlife." Communism teaches that this life is everything you have. But deep inside my soul, I knew something else was there, but couldn't pinpoint what it was.

One day I visited a cultural center where a speaker explained that to seek the truth you must answer first three basic questions: Who are you? Where did you come from? Where are you going?

Months went by, and one afternoon I told my mom I need to go to church. A neighbor invited me to visit a small run-down wooden Baptist church not too far from home. There, a hymn called "Holy Bible" was sung, and I heard these words: "Holy Bible, you are the truth; you tell me who I am, where did I come from, and where I am going to."

My heart stopped and the blindfold fell from my eyes. I saw Christ for first time and found the truth and the end of my quest.

Mario McDonald was born and raised in Cuba in 1963, came to the USA in 1995, and currently lives and works in Central Florida.

God Already Knew

By David McGan

I walked into the house from a business trip in early December of 2004. There, in a note on my recliner, was the message from my wife of almost thirty-two years that she had left me. This couldn't be happening. After all, our marriage was perfect; we were the model couple! But no matter how I tried to salvage our marriage, nothing worked, and the divorce became final five months later.

Throughout it all—the loneliness, despair, questions, and grief—I was given an even stronger faith that God was in control. My close friends and church family told me that God had something even better in store for me. And I found a peace that assured me that was true. So I waited on God.

At the same time, unknown to me, a lady who lost her husband to cancer in October of 2003 was facing the same type of despair, and was questioning why God would take her husband. But ultimately she prayed that if it be His will, God would send her a Christian husband. She was Catholic—very strong in her faith—but she neglected to specifically pray for a Catholic husband.

We met at a Christian Singles Dance in October 2005. I was only there to help a fellow Sunday school classmate get the organization started off. She was there with her widowed sister-in-law, thinking that her sister-in-law might meet someone, but not having the least amount of interest in looking for someone herself.

It turns out we both worked at the same company, so she thought at least we could talk at the dance, even though in her mind we had absolutely nothing in common. As time went on, we began to find that we had more in common than she thought.

Our love began to grow, but it took her a little while to say her suitable goodbyes to her husband and finally decide that she had come to love me deeply. In October of 2006, I asked her to marry me, and she said yes.

We've talked about it extensively; she and I both feel there were too many "coincidental" parallels in our lives that it had to be God's hand and His plan that resulted in His bringing us together. A song on a Hoppers album probably says it best, and has ministered to me greatly since I first heard it. The song? "God Already Knew."

We were married in April 2007 by her priest, had our reception at my Baptist church, and spent twelve days in Hawaii on our honeymoon. Today, we worship regularly together—and have since we started dating. She goes to Sunday school and church with me, and I go to mass with her.

My main desire through it all has been that I could be a witness to others. And God has even granted that. People have told me I handled the whole situation much more positively than they could have. I tell them it was God. A work colleague recently said how much he admired my Christian witness through it all. So God granted my desire—He already knew.

God has been so good to me. We don't always understand the direction our lives take, but I've come through this totally convinced that He's a Great God, and I could do no better than to just place my life and future totally in His Hands. That's where my wife and I are now.

David McGan lives with his wife, Mary Jane, in Corydon, Kentucky. He is a member of Immanuel Baptist Temple in Henderson, and Mary Jane is a member of St. Agnes Catholic Church in Uniontown. David also sings with a part-time southern gospel trio, The Echoes from Calvary.

The Miracle-Working Business

By Mary Messer

About two years ago our son, Scott, age forty-two at the time, had four strokes in eighteen months. The doctors said there was nothing they could do and sent him home. This past May, he had another one. He again went to hospital and was sent home in three days, the doctors telling him to see a stroke specialist. He could not get an appointment for two weeks.

The next day he had another one. We took him right to the stroke part of Harper Hospital, and it just so happened that the head of neuro-surgery was there. They took him right in. They did surgery by putting in two stints, one of which went to the brain, which had a seventy-five percent blockage. The other side had a one hundred percent blockage, but they could not do anything.

After surgery, his left side was paralyzed. He had slurred speech and loss of hearing in his ear. He was in rehabilitation at the hospital for two weeks. He was not able to move a finger. When he came home, he had therapy three times a week.

Now, nine weeks later, he is walking without a cane, his speech is okay, and his hearing is coming back. He is going back to work in about two weeks. God is surely still in the miracle-working business.

Mary Messer and her husband raised three sons in a Christian home. The family lives in DeFuniak Springs, Florida.

How Could I?

By Janetta Messmer

How could I have questioned His faithfulness? He'd shown it so many times in the years Ray and I were in business. I wondered why I doubted His ability this time.

Even before the doors of our shop opened, we felt the Lord leading us in that direction. The owner of the property we wanted to rent allowed us to pay the deposit over six months instead of all at once. The utility companies did the same. Parts stores opened accounts because they knew Ray's excellent reputation as a mechanic at other shops. The doors of opportunity opened, and we reaped the benefits.

From the first day we opened, customers flocked to our doorstep in need of car repairs. People who knew Ray trusted him. They knew he would do their job right. Also, our employees were told they'd follow our "honesty" philosophy or face the consequences—immediate termination.

The first year flew by. Our payroll met and our bills were paid on time. During the second year, we attended a course on running a business more efficiently. One of their classes taught us to save a percentage of our deposits each day.

The minute we returned home, I started transferring a percentage of each day's receipts into savings. Some days it didn't seem worth the trouble, but even a little bit added up. Within eight months we'd saved more than eleven thousand dollars.

Then in two short months, we found out why we'd been so diligent. Work at our shop died. Actually, every shop in town looked like a shop in a ghost town. But since we'd been faithful, we didn't worry.

The extra cash got us through the tough time. Our shop stayed open when others failed.

Ray and I thanked the Lord for the success of our business, but it didn't seem as though we could get ahead financially. Saving dwindled to every so often. My excuse was that there was never enough to go around, and something always needed to be fixed or replaced.

"We need *what* in four months for a new roof?" I asked my husband.

"We need sixteen thousand dollars. We knew it was coming. It's our responsibility," Ray answered.

"How are we going to do it?" Doubt clouded my mind. This might even be beyond the Lord's ability.

"It'll work out." Confidence rang out in Ray's voice. "Just keep praying and start saving."

Lord, it feels like someone served me an elephant and expects me to eat the whole thing in four big bites, I thought. *Where do I begin?*

I sensed Him telling me to start saving, which I began to do the next day. The money started to grow. Soon it became a game. Some days I'd put in extra and tell the Lord I trusted Him for the monies we needed. He never failed me.

"We did it," I yelled at Ray four months later.

"Did what?" My husband questioned.

"Saved the money for the roof. It's here." I showed him the bank book. "All sixteen thousand, Ray."

"I told you He'd do it." Ray smiled.

"Yes, but I didn't know He'd do it with such finesse." I sat, amazed at the Lord's faithfulness.

"Do not be anxious about anything, but in everything, by prayer and petition, with thanksgiving, present your requests to God. And the peace of God, which transcends all understanding, will guard your hearts and your minds in Christ Jesus" (Philippians 4:6b, 7, NIV).

Janetta Messmer lives in Spring, Texas, with her husband, Ray. They've been married for twenty-six years. Her publishing credits include "Making Marriage Work-While Working Together," featured in Guideposts Magazine *in July 2005.*

Joshua's Miracle

By Gaye Milam

When my son Joshua was six and a half months old, he began having seizures. We went to a doctor in Memphis. As we were going into the waiting room, Joshua began having a seizure. We were taken back immediately and the doctor came into the room and asked if I was his mother. I said yes, and he told us Joshua had tuberous sclerosis. This was a genetic disorder he had inherited from me. We knew the Lord took us to this doctor for a reason. The doctor told us because of the severity of Joshua's seizures, it was most likely that without treatment, he would be in a vegetative state within two weeks. The doctor told us medication could possibly help, but prayers and faith were also going to be needed. Some patients responded to the medication and some did not. What a miracle God had provided for us.

That very day we checked into LeBonheur Children's Hospital. The medication of ACTH (a steroid) was started and tests were done to check for tubers in other parts of his body. Small turbers were found on his brain and in his heart. We had to learn to give him the shot. We kept praying and kept our faith. We received another miracle. The medication worked. Joshua stopped having seizures.

Joshua is developmentally delayed because of the seizures and where the tubers are on the brain. With God's help, Joshua continued to improve, and he only had doctor's appointments once a year and CT scans every three to five years.

In July 2006, Joshua had to have a MRI on his brain. The MRI showed the tubers had grown and were blocking the drainage of the brain. He was sent to a doctor at Semmes-Murphy Clinic in Memphis. The neurosurgeon explained to us that he had tubers on each side of his brain. One was much larger than the other, and that was the one he said needed to be removed.

We set the surgery for August. Joshua was fourteen years old and facing brain surgery. We knew this was a major surgery, but we also knew the Lord was with us. Joshua was taken into surgery early on Tuesday morning. A portion of his skull had to be removed so the surgeon could perform the surgery, and then a titanium plate was put in. The surgeon said the surgery went great. He explained to us that he thought he got all of the large tuber and even thought he got the small one also. Praise the Lord, Joshua had done so well in surgery and both tubers had been removed.

On Thursday, the surgeon came in and told us that all of the larger tuber was removed, but he did not remove all of the smaller one. We were devastated. He said at some point it would have to be removed, but it was our decision whether or not to do the surgery now or wait until it grew. He said he could do the surgery on Friday, before Joshua's head started to heal. We prayed about the surgery, and God led us to have it on Friday. When the surgeon next talked to us, he had gotten all of the tuber out.

In March 2007, Joshua went for his six-month check-up; everything was great. We know God does perform miracles because He has performed so many in our lives. When I look at Joshua, I know he is a miracle from God. We give God all the praise and glory for all things that have happened in our lives. Isn't God good?

Gaye Milam lives in Charleston, Mississippi.

A Walking Miracle

By Lanay Money

My daughter and son in law have been married for about fourteen months. During that time, my son-in-law had a continuous battle with prescription medication, and as a result, he had been in and out of rehab centers. Nothing seemed to help.

My daughter stuck by him through it all. There were times when I just didn't see how she could go on anymore, but she always told me, "Mama, I live by two things. One, everything happens for a reason, and two, God will not put on me more than I can bear." Her faith has paid off. My son-in-law has been doing really well for the past few months and things are going well for them.

Another miracle in their life is my daughter is pregnant with a baby girl, Brenya Nichole, who is due October 24. My daughter has endometriosis, and the doctor told me when she was seventeen that there was a good possibility she might never have a child. Brenya is their miracle child, and Brenya's dad is a walking miracle.

I admire my daughter for standing beside her husband when things were at their worst. I want them to know I am so proud of both of them and am looking forward to becoming a grandma! God does still work miracles if we allow Him to.

Lanay Money and her husband Eddie live in Enola, Arkansas, with their two younger children, Cody and Ashley. They sing in the southern gospel group The Moneys. She is a paralegal and he is a travel nurse recruiter.

Dear Angels

By Carol Lynn Montgomery

How much different would my life be had I been raised in a God-fearing home? I'd like to think I would have done things differently.

I met the man of my dreams, made some bad choices, and found myself pregnant and almost dying from a miscarriage all in six months' time. With no one to talk to who understood what I was going through, I buried the pain as deep in my heart as I could, never quite succeeding. I got saved about eight years after I lost my baby, but my faith and understanding weren't strong enough to know how to give the Lord my grief. Two more miscarriages just added to this grief. I didn't know how to let go it. Even the birth of three healthy babies couldn't remove the grief and longing I felt.

I have blamed myself for more then twenty-five years for losing my three babies. I never got to hold them, never got to say I was sorry or I loved them.

There were no funerals, no closure. It hurt so much not to really know why they had to go, but finally with the Lord's help I found the courage to let them go.

When I sat down to write them a letter about all I was feeling it was a clear, sunny day in November. The hillside outside my window was muddy from recent rains. The Lord knew what was in my heart and the letter. While I sat there, the Lord gave me a vision of the hillside covered with fresh snow with three beautiful snow angels looking back at me.

I know the Lord did this to give me peace at last. I still miss them and cry, but I no longer feel the pain; I feel the comforting arms of the Lord.

This is part of my testimony I give when I introduce "Dear Angels," a song I wrote that came from the letter and God's love and healing. I share it with others so hopefully they can see they don't have to carry their grief endlessly; the Lord will gladly carry it for you and bring much-needed comfort. God's Love and Grace healed me so I could help others.

Carol Lynn Montgomery is a gospel singer and songwriter from Fleming County, Kentucky.

The Power of Prayer

Anna Rose Mooneyhan

Last August, my 54-year-old husband, Richard, was singing the last song in a southern gospel concert when he had a massive stroke. People rushed to help, and he was transported to the nearest hospital and put into the Neuro ICU. E-mails went out and his name was lifted in prayer by hundreds of folks.

After a week in the ICU, the critical care doctor determined he would need to have both a tracheostomy in his throat and a feeding tube for his stomach inserted on Monday. Surgeons were called in, and we were told that unless he regained his "gag reflex" by Monday, he would go to surgery. Until this time, I was unaware that to get off the ventilator, one must be able to gag. Two doctors and several nurses informed us that the "gag reflex" was one of the last things stroke patients get back. We immediately sent out the word for people to pray for this specific need. Our family constantly went to the Lord with this request all weekend, as we were afraid he would never be able to sing again if he had to have this surgery. On Monday morning, the critical care doctor came and began to check him out. He stood, looked surprised, and said, "I can't believe it, he's gagging!"

We were able to tell the doctor that people around the world had been praying for that one thing for him all weekend. What a testimony of God's grace and His power to answer prayers. After almost one year, nurses and doctors still remember us as the family that prayed and saw God move.

Richard is walking now with a cane, although he has no movement in his left hand or arm yet. He is still in physical therapy and is improving every week. He has begun to sing. And we're still praying and trusting God for complete healing.

Anna Rose Mooneyhan has been married to her husband Richard for thirty-seven years. They have four children and thirteen grandchildren.

Doing God's Will

By Robert C. Moyers

Halloween 1983: divorce was on the table. I had broken a commandment. I had hit bottom. I needed help. I cried out to God for help. The voice said, "You are the prodigal. Come home."

The next day—Saturday—I called my father and said, "May the prodigal son come home." He started to cry on the telephone and told me he had been praying for me. He said he had called Oral Roberts' Prayer Tower and asked for help. He then told me he had received a telephone call back. The person told him his prayer had been heard and soon he would receive a wonderful gift. There is no greater gift than the prodigal son returning home to his heavenly Father and his earthly father.

I wept. I made the decision to surrender my life to God and to do His will. I repented and rededicated my life to the Lord. I had known Jesus as Savior, but now I wanted to know Him personally as Lord, Master, Friend, and King.

The next day the war for control of my soul raged on. I was out of control. The battle between my selfish nature and my loving nature raged inside me. Again, I cried out for help. Suddenly the voice from inside me started to sing a song. "Oh little town of Bethlehem, how still we see thee lie. Cast out your sin, and enter in, be born again tonight."

Suddenly I was overwhelmed with inner peace. Some would say it was the peace that passes all understanding. Some would say it was the baptism of the Holy Spirit. There was no turning back. My focus on doing God's will each day had begun.

My twenty-fifth year of doing God's will has arrived. I serve God as president of the Center of Unconditional Love (COUL). I have also written a book, *Power of Peaceful Thinking: How to Know Jesus Christ as Savior, Lord, Master, Friend, and King.*

That's my story and I'm sticking to it.

Robert C. Moyers is president of the Center Of Unconditional Love and the author of Power of Peaceful Thinking: How to Know Jesus Christ as Savior, Lord, Master, Friend, and King. *He currently resides in Ohio.*

Two Hearts Beat to the Same Tune

By Frances Naff

My first cousin Teresa and I, along with our group, traveled and sang southern gospel music for thirty years. Our hearts beat to the same tune as we felt the calling of God on our lives in this field of our music ministry.

After our children were older and we were busy with our home lives, we decided to disband the group and spend more time with our families. She and I didn't see each other very often. Being closely related, we connected from time to time at family outings.

In the early part of this year, 2007, she was diagnosed with pancreatic cancer. She required surgery, chemo treatments, and several hospital stays. Many tests were needed to keep track of the progress of the cancer. I saw her several times during her illness, and each time my heart was grieving for her and her family, but I tried to remain cheerful and upbeat. Teresa always wore a great big smile on her face. And although her illness had taken its toll on her body, that sweet smile still remained.

Recently, she was hospitalized again for complications. The situation didn't look good. I asked her immediate family if I could visit with her. They are a family of precious, loving people—just like her—and they were glad I came.

Fighting back tears, I walked down the long hallway to her room. Several family members were standing by her bedside. When they told her I was there, she smiled really big, thrust her arms out, and welcomed me as I bent over to give her a hug. Looking at her, thoughts of our past music ministry and our closeness all those years resurfaced. I was overcome with hurt and had a terrible need to let go and scream! I glanced at the ceiling for a brief moment and sent up a quick prayer to God asking for calmness and the strength to say the right words to her.

Suddenly, a very strong voice came from my lips, and I said with an upbeat voice, "I've come to sing you a song, Teresa."

She weakly said, "Let's Sing."

Her son, sitting on the foot of her bed, smiled and said, "You wanna sing, Mama?"

She smiled again and told him she wanted him to lead one of her favorite old-time songs we used to sing a lot, "In My Robe of White." He started singing in his angelic voice, just like hers, as she and I joined in to give him harmony.

The family members gathered around her in the room were all amazed at her strength as she sang. I know only my heavenly Father could have kept the flooding of tears away from my eyes, and He gave us all an inner joy as heaven came down and glory filled our souls!

At this writing, she is still living and praising the Lord, and tells everyone that "God is in control."

Her legacy that she will leave behind is her contagious smile and her beautiful voice, but most of all, her love and praises to the most important person in her life, the Lord Jesus Christ!

I praise God for the thirty years we spent together; the many miles traveled; the albums and tapes we were blessed to record together; and for the joy, love, and happiness she always brought to my life.

Frances Naff has sung southern gospel music since she was ten years old. She is now sixty-four and a prayer coordinator for several different organizations. She is also a freelance writer, a wife, a mother of three, and a grandmother of four.

Two Songs

By E. Nafziger

In 2003, after a yearly checkup at my doctor's, it was deemed necessary for me to have a complete hysterectomy. Being anxious about the end result, a very dear friend forwarded to me a CD by The Isaacs which contained two songs, "Stand Still" and "He Understands My Tears." I nearly wore them out playing them over and over again. The result was that I was calm of soul and spirit while facing this surgery, and I received a clean bill of health. My family was more concerned than me. I thank God for their music and for the peace and calmness I received from listening. I have passed these two songs along to many friends and family.

Married for forty-seven years, E. Nafziger is a mother of four and a grandmother of six. Retired from a county service job, her many hobbies including reading, music, spending time with family and friends, and travel.

Another Family Miracle

By Richard Nash

The day was November 4, 1992. There was a terrible auto accident, in which two young men hit me head-on. It killed both of them, and they were sixteen and eighteen years old. They hit me head-on going about seventy-five miles per hour.

I was in the Palmyra Hospital in Albany, Georgia, for twenty-one days. The doctors told my mother and father I would not live. After I lived for a few days and they saw I wasn't going to die, they said, "Well, he lived, but he will never walk again." But once again they were wrong. I am walking, working, and trying to tell everyone what God has done for me. He truly is a miracle-working God, and as my mother has said many times, "He will do to depend on."

Richard Nash, age forty-nine, lives in Moultrie, Georgia, with his wife Lori. They have three children, ages twenty-seven, twenty-five, and twenty-three.

Healing Music

By Joyce Neely

Four times in my life, the Father has used music: to heal my fear of the death of my husband, to give certainty to a Chinese student that He created everything, to convince a Chinese student the words about God were true, and to heal emotional pain.

While listening to a concert in church, the Father was uprooting the fear of my husband's pending death from cancer. When I went home after the concert, I noticed the freight train coming down the track. I could not stop feeling he was totally gone. No, He did not heal my husband; He rescued him from ugly cancer by receiving him home.

While in China, I decided to play instrumental music with Scripture underneath it to my class. The nature sounds and music were very restful for the class. The bell rang; all left but one student. The Chinese student did not want to leave and said, "God made everything, didn't He?"

Another student had been given Christian music for his private hearing by another teacher. Two years later, he was part of a group who had accused the foreign teachers of saying things about God to their classes. He came to me and said, "I have decided that teacher was right. I believe in God, will you teach me?" Imagine the pleasure I had of telling him Jesus was the visibility of the invisible Father—God!

My spirit was so offended at a very immoral situation that I literally had pain on both sides of my spinal column. I could not touch my back with a blanket or lean back at church. I would duck mentally every time I thought of this immoral situation because I knew I would feel this very strong pain.

I went to a conference for women, and during the singing of the hymns something happened. Between verse one and four I sat down and cried, and then I got up and finished the last verse. The next morning when I looked for the pain, it was gone.

Joyce Neely is a school teacher from Erie, Pennsylvania, who is raising three kids. She has been retired from the Chinese spoken English classroom since 2001.

His Way Is the Only Way

By Nancy Nolan

As a preacher's daughter I grew up singing for the Lord, but as a teenager I felt I could do things my way. Of course, I made a terrible mess of my life without the Lord, and my children suffered for my mistakes. My oldest son was a skinhead who did drugs and was in much trouble. One night I dreamed of him in his coffin. What a wake-up call from the Lord!

I started to pray for my son, asked the Lord to be in control of my life, and haven't stopped praying yet. The Lord saved my son and all my children, and I am privileged to sing His praises and lead the children's choir in our small church. Now I know His way is the only way. Thank You, Jesus!

Born in Phoenix, Arizona, Nancy Nolan now resides in Huntsville, Alabama. She has four children, three step-children, fifteen grandchildren, and seven great-grandchildren.

God's Gift

By Ashley Rose Offenberger

I t was busy that day at work. When I left, I went directly to the babysitter's house to pick up my kids. They had been playing outside that day. They were ready for a bath. They were playing in the bath and I went to grab a diaper. When I came back I found my daughter under the water. She was blue all over. I got her out of the water. She had no pulse; she wasn't breathing. I immediately called 911. I explained the situation. They said someone would be right there. I knew what I had to do to help my little girl. Pray…pray…pray.

As soon as I started praying she immediately coughed up water, and I could hear my baby breathing. She was still lethargic, but she was breathing.

The first medical technician arrived and took her and started examining her. I could do nothing but stare at my little girl and keep praying. I kept thinking to myself, *How could this have happened when I was only gone a few seconds?*

They rushed her by air to the nearest hospital. The doctors were amazed at how well she was doing. All I could do was thank God for keeping my precious angel here with me. She is doing fine to this day.

I saw the medical technician not long after that. She told me, "I didn't want to tell you that night, but your daughter was dead. It was only God who kept your daughter here with you."

I had a hard time with the whole situation and with blaming myself. The doctors tried to explain that things like this happen and you have to keep all eyes on your children at all times, but I couldn't let go of blaming myself. But God gave me such a reassurance and peace, and only He got me through it. It was the hardest thing I have ever faced, but God brought me through and I am stronger today because of it. Praise the Lord!

Ashley Rose Offenberger lives in Floyd County in Virginia. She has a husband, Joseph; son, Johnathan; and daughter, Kaydin. The family attends Indian Valley Church of God.

In His Timing

By Sharon Ostrander

I have been a Christian for most of my life. In fact, I have stood by my husband's side for many years now as we've traveled all across the country in full-time ministry. I can remember seeing God work in spectacular ways many times throughout our ministry. I saw Him touch the lives of others when we prayed and believed Him. In fact, He would often do the impossible right before our eyes. Somehow it's different, though, to trust God for a need in your own life. Such was the case a few years ago.

God gave my husband and me a son. We named him Jeremy after the prophet Jeremiah. As you can imagine, he was and is the center of our lives. Early on he developed a severe ear problem. He would get tremendous ear infections which were accompanied by great pain that often brought him to tears. As you well know, watching your child hurt is difficult to do.

One night when he was only six years old, the pain got so bad that his eardrum burst and he was screaming in pain. We had taken him to the doctor earlier in the day, but nothing was working. After praying with what seemed like no results, my husband got upset with God. In fact, he left the room, and he later told me what he had done. He said he went into our bedroom, knelt down, and just told God how disappointing it was that He wasn't answering our prayers. In fact, he said he just told God he was never going to tell anyone ever again God was a healer if He wasn't going to hear our cries for help. As he knelt there, broken, hurt, crying, and disappointed, he had no way of knowing something was happening in the other room.

After countless prayers and several hours, Jeremy suddenly sat up and said, "Mom, I just felt the hand of God touch my ears!" He ran out of the room and into the bedroom where his Dad was kneeling on the floor by the bed, screaming, "Dad...the pain, it's all gone. It don't hurt anymore. Jesus just touched me. I felt Him touch me."

It seems that while we were angry with God, He was working in the other room in spite of our lack of faith in His timing. We learned a valuable lesson that night. God doesn't always show up in our time, but He does show up in His time, and in the meantime, it pays to be faithful and patient. God does answer prayer.

Sharon Ostrander is the wife of award-winning songwriter and singer Milton "Big Mo" Ostrander. She travels full-time with her husband and son all across America in ministry.

Abundance of Peace

By Jayeson Owen

"Behold, I will bring it health and cure, and I will cure them, and will reveal unto them the abundance of peace and truth." Jeremiah 33:6

Shortly before graduating Clemson University, I took an internship at a local state park. I was hired to direct all of the park's activities, including sports and guided hikes. I never finished this internship. Before the season got started, I had very itchy, strained eyes. I was using a bottle of eye drops a week. Next, I noticed when I would sneeze I would loose my eyesight temporarily.

It wasn't long before I woke up at my parent's house completely blind. They rushed me to an eye doctor, who agreed to meet with me in his office on Sunday morning. He could not figure out why I wasn't able to see. I was then rushed to the emergency room of the local hospital in Anderson, South Carolina. I wasn't there long before they realized they couldn't diagnose me either. I was then transported to Duke's Medical Center in North Carolina by ambulance. It was the longest ride of my life. By this point, I had been poked by more needles, including one directly into my back to test me for spinal meningitis. When I arrived at Duke, I was treated by Dr. Chestnut. His team eventually diagnosed me with bilateral optic-neuritis.

Now, very few people experience optic-neuritis (1 in 550,000 patients of multiple sclerosis). I have yet to find a doctor who has ever seen optic-neuritis bilaterally. Optic-neuritis is when the optic nerve swells. In my case, it swelled to the point of complete blindness. After my diagnosis I was placed on Prednisone, a steroid that would attempt to shrink the swelling.

The main reason the doctors were giving me this medicine was to attempt to relieve the incredible pain I was in. The doctors never gave me any hope of being able to see again.

One night while sitting in my hospital bed, I heard the words to a McKameys song that let me know I would see again. After hearing that song, I knew I would see again. It was at that moment God reached down and began a healing He has now brought to completion. I have perfect 20/20 vision and don't even need glasses.

My parents were by my side almost every second of my long hospital stay. Having them at that time in my life was such a blessing. I use to make my mom get so close to my face when I started to get my eyesight back because I missed seeing her. Today everyone always says things like "how scary!" or "you must have been scared to death!" It actually wasn't as scary as people think. I had such a peace the whole time I was blind. The only thing that ever bothered me was how it might affect my parent's lives. It was a long process, but now I have perfect 20/20 vision. The doctors may not understand…but I certainly do! You see, I am no stranger to grace.

Jayeson Owen resides in Tamarac, Florida. He is currently a special education teacher working with students who are mentally handicapped. He is also finishing his pastoral candidacy at Church of the Holy Spiritsong in Wilton Manors.

Angels in Overalls

By Norma Kennedy Patterson

My father was an avid hunter. Since moving to the Northwest from Illinois, the freezer was always well-stocked with venison. His faithful hunting companion all those years was my feminine little mother. I don't think she ever missed a year hunting with him, not because she loved hunting, but because she loved Dad.

A couple of years before the Lord gently took him to heaven at age ninety-three, Dad was still driving some and doing well, but when he insisted on taking his pickup and trailer and going hunting as usual that fall, we were apprehensive, to say the least. Neither my brother nor my husband was able to be away at that time, so I volunteered. If Dad was determined to go, at least someone would be with them.

We left Portland about midday and headed for Dad's favorite hunting spot near the coastal mountain range. We were well on our way when the weather suddenly became very stormy. Winds started gusting and shook the truck and trailer. It was raining hard and visibility was poor. It seemed that Dad was having difficulty seeing the gauges on the dash. Mom was calm, as usual, but I knew she was praying. Her faith was dauntless.

As darkness began to fall early, the winds increased, and likewise, so did the tightness in my stomach. My dad had always been so competent, but he was past ninety and I was petrified! Then, as I silently prayed, I began to visualize angels—on the hood of the pickup, on top of the camping trailer, in the cab with us—and I began to relax. The exit sign ahead told us we were ready to turn off the main highway, still miles from our destination.

Immediately after we turned off the freeway, everything suddenly turned black. Our headlights had stopped working! Dad was able to park the truck and trailer in a safe place, well off the side of the highway. He tried to find the problem with the headlights, but they just wouldn't work. He finally decided the Lord was trying to tell him something! We spent the night in the trailer and headed back to Portland the next morning under sunny skies.

Later, when my husband investigated the problem with the lights, everything was working perfectly and still doing fine when Dad sold his pickup a year later. Those guardian angels were certainly clever at disabling Dad's headlights just long enough to let him know it was time to head home!

Norma Kennedy Patterson and her husband live in a suburb of Portland, Oregon. He is a retired auto body technician and she is a retired nurse anesthetist. They both love gospel music.

Airport Angels

Joyce Payne

Several years ago, my son and myself were on a flight from Atlanta to Los Angeles/Madera, California, when my son suddenly became ill with a virus. The flight attendants were very helpful, but there I was on a flight with no way to get off and a sick child. I was so upset, wondering what I was going to do. We had to make connections, get a rental car when we reached our destination, and drive twenty miles. When we landed in Los Angeles, I was approached by a couple who stated they were seated nearby us on the aircraft and had noticed my son was sick.

I was startled, because I did not recall seeing them in Atlanta or on the plane. They asked if they could be of help to me. The gentleman was kind enough to go and check on my son in the bathroom. They stayed with me while we were waiting for our next flight. I asked them where their destination was and they said Fresno, and they were renting from Avis Car Rental also. I still am startled by what I experienced. They helped me get my luggage on the trolley to the rental car office, went in with us to pick up our car, and then disappeared. Did I ask their names? No! At any other time, I would have gotten their names and where they were from. I truly believe I was entertaining angels unaware. I'm so glad we serve a God who can take care of any situation, whether we are at home, 3,500 miles from home, or flying 35,000 feet in the air.

Joyce Payne is an office manager at First Baptist Church in Oneonta, Alabama. She currently resides in Altoona and is married and the mother of one son.

An Unexpected Blessing

By Dana Pelno

Last year right before Christmas, I needed some money for an unexpected bill. I had no clue where it would come from, as I was on disability and bankrupt. When I got sick in 1998, I missed a whole year of work, and that would put anyone in a really deep hole financially.

I prayed and prayed and asked the Lord for a miracle. During the whole time I was trying to think of a way to get the money. You know how that is; I'm sure you have done it also.

For all of my life I had worked at least two if not three jobs at a time; taken care of my mother, who had been ill ever since her forties; and did all the weddings at my church, including decorating, directing, and even singing for them. The very first one I did was for a dear friend and she and her husband, and I have remained friends with them all these years. They wanted to do something for me gift-wise for doing their wedding. Her mother did not help her at all, and I basically was her Mother, going with her to try on dresses and doing all the stuff you have to do in preparation for a wedding. Anyway, she started to make me something (a surprise), and I never got it. I never thought a thing about it. I made her blankets when she started to have children.

Lo and behold, the Lord moved them to Roanoke for his job, and we had lost touch over the last couple of years. One day the mail lady came to the door with a certified letter for me. All I could think of was that it was another bill. Instead, it was a letter from them saying they were so sorry they had not gotten my gift to me all those years ago, but that it was probably a good thing because they wouldn't have been able to do what they were doing now. They have been married for twenty-four years, and inside one of their wedding napkins from way back when was a check to me for five hundred dollars. I nearly fell down! Twenty-four years later, a gift of money, which was what I needed, came from the most unexpected place I could ever imagine! Who else but God could do that right on time? Can you believe it?

I cried and cried and praised the Lord over and over and sent them a long thank-you letter explaining how I had prayed and needed money and had no clue where it was going to come from and how the Lord used them to answer my prayer. Hallelujah!

God is so awesome. I mean, never in my wildest dreams would I have ever thought of that source as being an answer to my prayer. Talk about out of the blue! Anyway, I hope you will join me in letting God fix our problems and then join me in singing a chorus of "Praise God, From Whom All Blessings Flow!"

Dana Pelno currently resides in Richmond, Virginia.

A Fighting Chance

By Dixie Phillips

My husband and I were overjoyed at the birth of our second child, John Drake Phillips, on October 27, 1980. He was born with a black eye, and we joked about him one day being our heavyweight fighter. Little did we know that in just two short weeks, he would be in a fight for his life.

On John's two-week birthday, he woke up whimpering like a sick puppy. I went over to his crib to see what was wrong. He wouldn't open his eyes, but his high-pitched whimper continued. I attempted to nurse him, but had no success. We immediately took him to the doctor. The doctor didn't waste any time telling us that John must be admitted to the hospital. My husband and I were in a state of shock. How did our baby get so sick? After several tests were run, a pediatrician came to visit with us. He was very somber and informed us that they believed John had contracted spinal meningitis. There was a good possibility John might die. Our hearts beat wildly. The doctor explained that if they could get the fever to break, we might have a chance of saving our little boy.

Over the next twelve days, my husband and I would take turns spending the night at the hospital. One night, on my watch, John's fever continued to rage. I stood by his bed and pleaded with him to not give up. About that time a nurse came in and turned *The 700 Club* on. A gospel group was singing. I began to cry uncontrollably. The presence of God had come into that hopeless place. One of the singers said they had a Word from the Lord, "There's a newborn baby boy who is very sick in the hospital." I sat there stunned as the singer continued, "The walls of the hospital room are green."

I quickly looked at the hospital walls, and they were green.

"The doctors have told you that your little boy might not live, but God wants you to know that this sickness is not unto death. Your baby boy is going to live."

They went on to finish the song. As they sang the final chorus, a peace swept over my being. I knew John was going to live. I knew God was going to heal our little boy. I raised my hands and began to thank God for John's healing. I knew I was standing on holy ground and that God was granting us a miracle. That very night John's fever broke.

The next day the doctor came in and was guarded as he spoke. "John has had a high fever for several days. He is going to live, but he might have brain damage."

No fear gripped my heart. No "what ifs?" captured my soul. I had experienced a visit from heaven and I knew John was healed. Five days later we took our baby boy home completely whole.

John is now twenty-six years old. We reminisce often of the day Jesus passed by and healed him. We are convinced John wouldn't have had a fighting chance of survival without a supernatural touch from heaven, even if he was born with a black eye.

Dixie Phillips and her husband have pastored the Gospel Lighthouse Church for twenty-six years. They have four grown children. They are promoters of the annual Floyd Iowa Gospel Sing held every September. Dixie enjoys ghostwriting.

An Amazing Grace Story

By Dale Pittman

On Father's Day, June 17, 2007, my mother, Nadine Pittman was in CCU in an Abilene, Texas, hospital following a massive heart attack and life support was stopped at 2:15 p.m. My wife and two daughters could not be there until 7 p.m. since my oldest daughter, who was eighteen years old, was on a "Walk to Emmaus."

Upon their arrival at the hospital, I met them out front and explained to them what they would see when they walked into Mom's room so they would not be shocked. Mom was only on oxygen and a morphine drip to keep her comfortable.

After we all had been in the room and our entire family had regained some composure, my eighteen-year-old daughter, Jessica Marie, started singing "Amazing Grace." We were all around Mom's bed holding hands, and we sang two verses through our tears to her. At the end of the singing, Jessica walked up closer to her "granny," leaned down and gave her a kiss, and told her, "Granny, we are going to be okay. Don't worry about us, as we will be together a lot longer than we will be apart."

One hour and ten minutes later my mother took her last earthly breath and stepped into the awaiting arms of our loving and awesome Savior. For the first time in three and a half years, Mom was no longer struggling to breathe, as she was healed, and now awaits us to join her on those golden streets of heaven.

On the way back to Big Spring, Texas, where we live, Jessica Marie and her sister, Jennifer, were driving home and were involved in a one-car accident, hitting a guardrail almost head on. Praise the Lord neither one was injured except for some minor bruises and soreness. I told my daughters their "granny" had already become their guardian angel. Had the guardrail not been there, the outcome would have been fatal, so we praise God for His amazing grace.

Dale Pittman resides in Big Spring, Texas.

My Precious Miracle

By Veronica Plunkett

In 2001, I tried to take my own life. I thought no one cared about me. I was admitted to a mental hospital for three days. Boy, was I wrong! First off, not only did my family love me more than I realized, but Jesus also loved me more than I could ever imagine! He told me straight out that He was not ready for me yet, and I did have a reason to be here on earth.

I was thirty-one then; I'm thirty-seven now and have a beautiful, precious three and a half-year-old daughter! I was pregnant with twin girls and due in May of 2004. However, I went into labor on Valentine's Day. When I first found out I was pregnant, the doctor wanted to abort my one twin girl. I wouldn't let him do it. I told him it was not my decision, it was God's! I had an emergency c-section that night at 7:45 p.m. My one girl weighed 2 lbs. 2oz. and was 13.3" long; we named her Charity Grace. Our other daughter was 1 lb. 5 oz. and 13" long; we named her Angel Dawn. They were both born very premature.

Charity was a lot healthier than Angel. Angel got to be here for sixteen days. She passed away on March 1, 2004. We did get to spend some time seeing her and were able to get some pictures while she was here with us. Charity had to stay in the hospital until May 29, 2004. She came home and was on oxygen for three months. Now she is just as healthy as any baby that was carried full-term.

Instead of being bitter toward God for taking Angel, we thank Him everyday for Charity! Charity has made me realize she is one reason

God wanted to keep me here on earth. God answered my prayer—I'm a mommy now!

Veronica Plunkett is a 37-year-old woman who has been married to a 50-year-old man for almost six years. They have a daughter and live in Linden, Tennessee. The family attends New Life Christian Church.

From Darkness to Light

By Russell Pruitt

I had no church upbringing. Dad was an alcoholic, and he and Mom divorced when I was fifteen. I started playing drums in bar bands when I was sixteen and kept on playing clubs after high school, and I did it full-time until I was thirty.

In 1971, a Hindu swami became my guru. I had been married to a beautiful girl for six years and had a five-year-old son. After living with a musician who became a yogi, my wife had the good sense to divorce me. I moved into the Yoga Ashram, was given a Hindu name, and took vows to become a monk. There was a Bible in our library, as well as holy books of all the world's religions, and I started reading the psalms and gospels. Then a former bandmate of mine came over and started witnessing to me about Jesus. I began to be very interested in this Jesus, because He seemed to be unique among all the founders of religions, having been raised from the dead. But this was a problem, because I still loved my guru.

Circumstances led me back to my hometown for what I thought would just be a short visit. I wanted to teach my family about Yoga, so they said I could teach them Hatha Yoga (the physical exercises) if I would go to church with them. It may be hard to believe, but I don't remember ever having heard a gospel sermon. I was fascinated with the preaching, and the more I heard, the more I wanted to hear. It seemed Jesus was claiming by a simple act of His will that He could give me all those spiritual graces I had been working so hard for all those years. I was used to performing religious rituals to obtain favor from God, but all Jesus asked was that I admit to being a sinner, and ask Him for forgiveness.

I really didn't feel like a sinner because I had been trying to work my way to God for years by meditation, asceticism, and service to humanity, but one Sunday morning I thought to myself, "I really want to make Jesus my guru, and it wouldn't hurt to say 'I'm a sinner, please forgive me.'" Before my knees hit the floor, the Jesus that I had been reading and hearing about became real to me. In a moment of time, He revealed Himself to me and took me as His own, delivering me from heathenism and idolatry.

For the last thirty years I have tried and failed to plumb the depths and scale the heights of that initial experience. I know I never will. In less than a year, He saved my then ten-year-old son, and not much later, He saved my wife. We were remarried twenty-nine years ago, my son serving as my best man. The Lord also gave us a beautiful girl. He helped me get two degrees, called me to preach, and gave me a career as a social worker. Eight years ago, He decided to make me a songwriter. To His glory, I have co-written a song with John Rowsey on Hope's Call's *Live to Love* album. Another one of my songs won first place in a gospel songwriting contest, and I had another song place as a finalist in this year's CMT/NSAI song contest. Six hundred thousand words couldn't tell the miracles He has done for me.

Russell Pruitt is married to Carolyn. They live in Portsmouth, Ohio, and have two grown children and a granddaughter. Pruitt is a social worker, bi-vocational Baptist minister, and a lifetime Musician Union member. He is also a songwriter and a Regional Songwriter's Workshop coordinator for NSAI.

The Gospel Group

By Judy Purkey

After attending church one Sunday, my husband Jack told me God had showed him a vision while in church. He said the Lord was calling him to play a guitar in a gospel group. Being shy, he didn't want to do this, so he convinced himself this was something he just had on his mind. A few weeks later, God showed him who the lead singer was in a dream, and that he wanted to be in the group with him.

Let me show you how awesome God is. One Sunday morning after the dream, Jack and I were going to a different church than the one we usually attended. Before we left, Jack told me who the lead singer was in his dream, but he told me to not say anything about this to anyone. He said that if God was in this, He would take care of it.

When we got to church I sat down beside our friend Rosemary, and Jack sat on the other side of me. Not long after the service started, Rosemary whispered to me and said, "I feel like someday I will be singing and Jack will be playing the guitar in a gospel group." I knew God could do great things, but I was still shocked. This was the woman Jack had told me the Lord showed him just before we left the house. I told her what Jack had said just before we left home. Then the group started forming. I hadn't told her who else God had showed Jack would be in the group. And she went and asked this same person.

Jack said, "The rest of them had their backs to Him in the dream." But God brought them in as they kept praying about this. We all know God put his approval on this group because they were never without a place to sing and mainly because souls were saved and lives rededicated. Praise the Lord!

Judy Purkey and her husband, Jack, currently reside in Mooresburg, Tennessee.

A Lifetime Commitment

By *Jan Raisen*

In 1965, after my high school graduation, the man I fell in love with completed his four years in the service and wanted to return home. In hope of a future with him, I traveled to his state of New York and set up residence there. After about a year, a rumor surfaced that he wanted to date other girls but did not want to be the one to break it off and hurt me. So with much pain I asked if it was true. Without his denying the rumor, I suggested we go our separate ways and decided to return home. I had hoped he would ask me to stay. He didn't. My life felt in limbo for a while.

On the rebound, I married another man. Three children and nineteen years later we divorced. I had dreams throughout my life regarding the man I truly loved. They were always the same. I was standing on a bridge looking down. He would be standing on the bank looking up at me. I could never touch him, but he was always there.

After my divorce, I went to visit him as we had promised each other we would touch base at some point in our lives. He was very distant, but kind and happy to see me. He took me to see the World Trade Center building. It was a nice visit, but I returned home with the same pain I had left with nineteen years prior.

Thinking I would never see him again, I remarried. I had one child with my second husband, and then thirteen years later I was widowed. I absorbed myself in singing gospel songs and grew deeper in the faith. That seemed the only thing that could bring me through another day. I so enjoyed singing that I decided to make a CD for my children and friends at church. I sent one to the man I had loved so many years earlier. I think it was my way of letting him know I was okay with there being no strings attached.

I started dating another man and got engaged, but things didn't seem right. The Lord was working on something and I knew it, but I had no clue what this was.

On September 11, 2001, the World Trade Center was destroyed. I thought all the world was crumbling. Things were not working out with my fiancée. Well, one week after 9/ll, I got a phone call. Even then I didn't know what the Lord was doing. It was my friend from the past. He said he was calling to see if it was me he took to see the World Trade Center. During our conversation, we could both feel the Lord working. Having been single all his life, my longtime love was praying for a Christian wife at the age of sixty-two. He was ready for a lifetime commitment. After several signs from the Lord, we both knew this was from Him and married ten months later. Jesus knew we were not ready for each other until now. We have been married five years now and the Lord just keeps working and blessing us with His love and the love we have for each other.

Sometimes I think about how sad 9/11 was, but our story is a happy one. 9/11 brought us together. I thank God every day for the good Christian man I have. I stand in awe of how He works. This is my personal praise.

Jan Raisen is a mother of four and a grandmother of fourteen. She is now retired and serves her church in various ways. She sings in the choir, teaches Sunday school, and is the new mission president.

Each Breath Is a Miracle

By Jerry Reed

God has been so good to me. Where do I start? Each day I awake—or I should say each breath I breathe—is another blessing and another opportunity to praise God.

At age three I found out I was born with a defective aortic heart valve. I am now forty-four, and I have had three open heart surgeries and an aortic heart valve replacement. The doctors labeled me a high risk heart patient and my activities have been limited my whole life.

I praise God that I was raised in a Christian home and always believed in God and the miracles He could perform. He has performed many on me. Just being alive is an answer to prayer, and I praise God for it daily. You see, I have had the same heart valve in me for twenty-seven years as of this writing in 2007. It is a miracle I am here today, and each breath from God is another miracle from Him. Even though I have had many setbacks and problems since 1980, when the valve was replaced, God has always seen me through them all. He is an ever-loving God, and every miracle has come from Him.

I also battle with bipolar disorder, which is very difficult to me and my friends and family. But, once again, only through the grace of God can I get through it. It takes a lot of prayers and trusting totally in Him to get through it all. What a great God we serve!

Doctors are amazed at how well I am doing, and many times they don't understand it. It is then that I can share with them it is God who is performing miracles in me through the power of prayer. I have been in the singing ministry for thirty-plus years, and it is still a very moving time for me when I get to share my testimony. I pray it touches hearts and helps someone along the way.

Jerry Reed resides in Dexter, Missouri. He has traveled and sung southern gospel music with several different groups, and he has also done a solo ministry.

Trusting God Even When You Don't Understand

By Patricia L. Reich

Having trials and hardships are a part of life, and I can't avoid them. But having God with me through them makes all the difference.

N January of 2001, I had multiple reactions to an antibiotic. My doctor was not available, so I saw another. He prescribed me an antibiotic I had taken before for a sinus infection, but it was much stronger. I soon felt better until after I took my last pill. I developed a severe reaction to the medication.

It was a Sunday morning, and I was getting ready for church when hives and bad chest pains started. I called the Tel-A-Nurse of my situation and she advised me to immediately call an ambulance.

If it was not for God, I would have freaked out. From the beginning, I gave Him my concerns and frailties, and He gave me His strength and comfort. I had such a peace and calmness through it all. After exam and tests, I was given Benadryl for the itching and a special cocktail for severe acid reflux, which was causing the chest pains. The antibiotic was hard on my hiatal hernia. They said I had an allergic reaction to penicillin.

Within a week or so, I was back in the hospital with severe pain and unable to function properly. Upon doing blood work, they found my reaction to the antibiotic had set off another reaction, which was rheumatoid arthritis. It was the worse pain I ever experienced in my life. I was given another antibiotic for infection and something for the pain. I was concerned about taking pain pills, so I took extra strength Tylenol instead. I leaned upon God to get me past the pain, which He did. He stayed with me through it all. The rheumatoid arthritis lasted more than two weeks. My husband, a friend, and a neighbor cared for me.

God prepared me beforehand through a Bible study our church provided, which was called "A Heart Like His." One particular part was on "Further Still," which she described as a place you go to where you have a real closeness and intimate time of fellowship and sweet communion with God. I longed to go there and find that place. I know this study was part of God's plan for me. During my confinement in bed, there were many times when God whispered "Further Still" to me. I can't explain how much comfort that gave me. Even in pain, I was basking in sweet communion with God. What a wonderful place to be. With limited mobility and weakness, I learned to depend and lean upon God. Whenever I needed His help or direction, He was there for me. I will never be able to comprehend the power and presence of God, but I know of His loving kindness and caring ways. I can have joy in the Lord even in the most difficult times.

My final reaction was treatment of thrush. We were into March before I recovered and gained my strength back. I could not have gone through this traumatic experience without God by my side. I am thankful God used this opportunity to take me to that place of "Further Still." I am not worthy of His love, grace, and mercy, and still, He extends it to me. How I love Him. He is my dearest Friend.

Patricia L. Reich lives in New Columbia, Pennsylvania, with her husband and their Shih Tzu. She enjoys listening to southern gospel music.

Jesus Will Always Be There for You

By Cathy J. Reynolds

I awoke from a very real dream one night, telling my husband about it. In the morning, there on my night stand, was a note I had written. It said, "I was to do a concert at a place called Westminster Village on a Wednesday night. I was to let a man named Charlie know he was not alone, was loved, and that Jesus would always be there for him." I told my husband; I had to be obedient to GOD and do it.

Two weeks later I located the retirement village and contacted the activities director, who said the only opening was Wednesday night. I said, "I'll take it." My husband asked if a Charlie lived there. She said the only Charlie was a man who just moved in a couple of days before, and that he was not doing well. His wife was ill and would probably have to be put in the nursing home part of that community. She said she would make sure he knew of the concert. I said that if God wanted me to do the concert for him, He would make sure to have Charlie there.

I did the concert, and it was so well received I could feel the presence of God all around me. I ended with the song "Jesus Will Always Be There for You," which the Dove Brothers' Jerry Kelso wrote for me after I told him of finding a dollar bill with the words written across it at a time I needed to hear them most. Hoping Charlie got the message, I said thank you and ended the show, at which point my husband walked up, took the microphone, and asked for Charlie. I had not done this, as I didn't want the rest of the people in the audience to think I wasn't there for them. No one said a word. He then added, "Does anyone know a Charlie or a Chuck?"

A little lady about halfway back stood up and said, "I know a Charlie who lives across the hall from me. He isn't doing well. He won't eat, talk, or even come out of his room! His wife died two days ago."

Silence fell over the entire room; we were near tears. Then a man stood up and said, "I didn't know we had a man here named Charlie, I am going to go meet him."

A lady stood up and said, "What do you mean he won't eat? I am going to take him some cookies I baked today."

Another lady said, "Let's go see him right now and take him a CD of that song."

One after another, people came up to me and asked if I had a message for him. I said, "Yes. You tell Charlie Jesus will always be there for him. Tell him he is not alone. Although he just moved here and knows no one, he now has all of you."

The next morning the lady in charge of activities called and thanked me for being obedient. Charlie was eating, talking, and did attend the funeral with his new friends at his side. I was honored to be a part of God's hand at work. You see, I thought I was to sing to Charlie, but I was just a vessel to get him the friends he needed to help him heal.

Cathy J. Reynolds was awarded Southern Gospel Artist of the Year for independent Christian artists in Nashville, 2006 and 2007. Her shows feature inspirational, patriotic, and spirited southern gospel style. She resides in Morton, Illinois, with her husband, Vern.

Just in Time

By Eunice Rice

My daughter is a rural postal carrier. I always pray for God to keep her safe, especially in the winter time on the snow and ice. A couple of years ago, we had a severe ice storm, but you know the mail must go on. Anyway, as usual I prayed for God to protect her and keep her safe while driving around on the ice delivering mail.

After her route was over, she called me to let me know how it went. It turns out, while coming up to a stop sign at a major highway, her car hit a patch of ice and started sliding and slid right into the path of a tractor-trailer truck. We all know how hard it is for a tractor-trailer to stop, but while she was telling me about it, God gave me a vision of His hand reaching down and stopping that truck. I looked up and said, "Thank You, God, for answering my prayer this morn. I give You the praise, honor, and glory for everything."

Our God is an awesome God and He always answers prayers right on time. I have many stories to tell of what He's done for my family and me, but this one was absolutely awesome and just in time. The tractor-trailer driver stopped so fast that I'm sure he's still probably trying to figure out how that happened. Other than being totally shaken up, my daughter returned to the post office that day safe, even when, on the way back to the post office, a tall, slim pine tree fell across the top of her car.

Eunice Rice has lived in Eden, North Carolina, her entire life. She has three children, nine grandchildren, and one great-granddaughter.

The Day My Life Changed Forever

By Rachel Ann Richardson

It was February 11, 1999. It was just like any other day. I was your typical nineteen-year-old. I went to work, hung out with my closest friends, and spent time with my family, never thinking that at any time my life could change forever.

That night I went to work like I usually did and was told to come home in the middle of my shift because there had been an awful accident. The sheriff called and said my seven-year-old sister had been killed in an automobile accident. I couldn't even breathe; it was like someone had kicked me in the stomach and I fell to the floor. It didn't seem real. We lived in a small town and stuff like that just didn't happen. I didn't know how I would ever make it through without her. She was one of my closest friends.

It turns out God had something else in mind for our family. The only survivor of the accident was my fifteen-month-old baby cousin. They life-flighted him to the children's hospital. After not knowing whether he would make it through the night or not, he is now a very healthy nine-year-old and the biggest blessing to our family. He is my new brother since his mother was killed in the accident. My parents also now raise him as their own, and we couldn't imagine life any differently.

Ashley, my seven-year-old sister, will always have a special place in our heart and will always be missed, but it was also a gift from God to have a very special boy added to our family. He is what brought us through our tragedy. This is how God works in miraculous ways. One tragedy turned into a blessing. Without God in my life, I would be nothing. He has gotten me through every valley and been there with me on every mountain. No matter how big or small the case may be, He is always there to call upon.

Rachel Richardson is twenty-seven years old and lives in Grand Island, Nebraska, with her husband David and their three children, Gracey, Garrett, and Gabrielle.

The Wheelchair Section

By Clementine Riddell

My story starts at the NQC convention of 1994 in Louisville, Kentucky. I think it was our second time attending the convention. That year we decided to become permanent seat holders for Thursday-Saturday starting the next year, which would be 1995.

In August of 1995 my husband and I went to Florida for my parents' fiftieth wedding anniversary. We didn't stay as long as we had planned and came back early. I think it was two days later I decided to go to Richmond, Kentucky, and do some shopping. As I was driving I heard the words "slow down" twice, so I slowed down. I drove about four or five more miles, and as I came around this curve I saw a car in the other lane run off the road and onto the shoulder twice. I thought to myself they must be drunk. Then the car straightened up back on the road and I thought things were all right.

All of a sudden, the car was coming right at me. There was nowhere for me to go to get of the way. I said, "Oh God, they're gonna hit me," and they did. I remember the crash and the next thing I remember was my Chevy blazer turning over on its side. As it was turning over, I felt myself falling to the passenger side of the car. As I was falling I could feel two hands on either side of my face, just letting me fall gently as I fell against the window. The person who hit me was pregnant and had fainted while driving. We had our left foot broken, and we had a lot of bruises and small cuts.

This happened in the last week of August and the NQC convention was in September. The time came for the convention, and I was in a wheelchair. I was not supposed to put any weight on my foot for six weeks.

175

My husband and I went to the NQC on Thursday night, having no idea where we would be sitting. We found an usher to show us where we'd be sitting. She took us through a doorway and said, "You'll be sitting in the handicapped area for wheelchairs." I didn't know what to say. She then looked at me and said, "Did you know you were going to be in a wheelchair?"

I said no. I knew God did though. It was just another time for Him to let me know He'd take care of everything. He knows how. I thought this was really awesome. Of course we serve an awesome God! Oh, we're still sitting in the same seats; of course I'm not in the wheelchair section now.

Clementine Riddell will have been married to her husband Tony for forty years in October. They have two grown boys. They have been singing gospel for fourteen years. They live in Irvine, Kentucky.

Hannah's Prayer

By LeAnn Romine

My husband and I had been praying for a fourth child. We already had three biological children, but due to circumstances beyond our control we were unable to have more children. As this desire began to grow, I became discouraged and felt hopeless. The one late Sunday night I was led to 1 Samuel, and this changed everything. I began reading about a young woman who had the same desire as me.

Hannah wanted a child so desperately, and she cried out to God for that child. I could identify with Hannah. I also wanted my fourth child desperately, and I had cried out to God many times. When I read 1 Samuel 1:27, something rang out in my spirit! "For this child I prayed; and the Lord hath given me my petition which I asked of him." Hannah had cried out to God, and He answered her!

At the time, adoption still seemed impossible because of the cost, but from that night on I began thanking God for our fourth child. At times, it sounded ridiculous thanking God for a child we didn't even have. When discouragement would try to hit, I would hold on to 1 Samuel 1:27 and just continue to thank Him. Four years had passed and still nothing.

Then one October evening in 2002 we received a very unexpected phone call. A relative in my family who was a very young teen mom was no longer able to care for her child. She contacted a social worker and requested that we take this child and raise him as our own. We were very surprised she had chosen us for this awesome responsibility of raising this child.

We had to complete an adoptive home study, and by March of 2003 we had a little three-year-old boy in our family. Our adoption was completed in June of 2004. I'm not really sure how I had expected God to bring us a fourth child, but this was definitely a surprise and not what we had expected. I had ruled out adoption due to the cost, but the adoption of our little boy was almost completely covered.

God answered our prayer! I would encourage any couple who is praying for a child to read about Hannah in 1 Samuel. Hold on to the precious desire God has given you and don't give up. Even when things look impossible in the natural, God can still bless people in such unexpected ways.

LeAnn Romine has been married to her husband John for nineteen years. She is a stay-at-home mom who is raising four children, Katie, Nichole, Melissa, and Devon. They currently reside in Cedar Rapids, Iowa.

A Two-Fold Blessing

By John W. Roth

I t was a Saturday afternoon; I was working in my shoe store in Poway, California. I had just gone next door to Albertsons to buy a fresh pack of cigarettes. I came back and settled in for my afternoon break to have a smoke. I was a Christian Sunday school teacher and youth leader who had un-dealt with habits. I had brought with me a cassette tape my wife had given me of a service I had missed. I popped it into the cassette and was preparing my pack of cigarettes. The preacher's message was not clear to me until later, but it was very interesting. He was making a noise as if he was flicking a Bic cigarette lighter, and he gave what I believed was a lesson on smoking and Christian service. As I listened, the flicking was getting louder. With that noise and the message I was hearing, God was convicting my heart. On September 1, 1992, I took that brand new pack of cigarettes, wadded them up, and threw them away for the last time.

I did not tell my wife for about three days because I had lied in the past about quitting. I would go to the altar at church, praying God would take away my habit, and then pick up the cigarettes and walk out to light up once I got home. My heart had not bee in tune with God's.

The fact was, my wife already knew I had quit because I no longer smelled like a smoke stack. It was on a Tuesday evening when I decided to tell my wife about the blessing God had given me, the fact that He had taken my cigarettes away, and how I had not had one in three days. As I proceeded to tell her about the cassette tape, tears were flowing down her cheeks. I said, "Dear, why are you crying?"

My wife's next statement to me was my confirmation: "John, that was not a Bic cigarette lighter the pastor had; it was a rose bush, and the pastor had a pair of sheers and was cutting the thorns off the rose bush. He was giving the lesson of how God saves us and then molds us in His time into what He wants us to be by taking the thorns (rough edges) off our lives."

God had touched my heart that day, for it was in His time He provided me with His blessing. God took this burden away fifteen years ago, which leads into the two-fold blessing—praise God He is still answering prayer.

John W. Roth is a 54-year-old retired Navy chief. He has been married to Susan for thirty-four years. They have seven children and seven grandchildren. They are members of Mill Creek Baptist Church in St. Augustine, Florida.

Blessed Through Cancer!

By Carol Sanguinette-How

I n 1996, I was informed I had breast cancer! At that time, my thoughts included: "My life is a very happy life! There have been some very hard knocks, but a faithful God has always brought me through. My life is filled with God's love and grace, my family, music, and my work! I am a secretary at a public school district. I teach Sunday school and sing at various churches and at a variety of activities. I cannot believe I will be forty-eight in September! Where have these years gone? I do not have time to be sick with anything, much less cancer!"

My cancer was an estrogen-fed cancer. So when I had finished with thirty-six radiation treatments, I was scheduled for a complete hysterectomy. That did not disappoint me at all. What did disappoint me was that I was going to have to have chemotherapy after all. I had been told early on that since the cancer was not in my lymph nodes, I would not need chemo. I was truly devastated, but for only about twenty-four hours! Then I realized God was so good and He had it all under control and in His plan. I was meeting wonderful people, my new family; cancer survivors know that family. They are the family we don't want to belong to, but become connected with anyway.

When I found out about the chemo, I decided to get my hair cut really short (I had lots and lots of hair). If I was going to lose hair, I'd lose little, short pieces instead of long pieces. Guess what? Six months and many treatments later, I still had hair. My oncologist had emphasized, "You *will* lose your hair!" Wrong! As vain as it may seem, I was so thrilled that the doctor had been wrong about just that one thing! I was so happy to still have my hair!

The chemo was tough, but five months after beginning the treatments and eighty-six Neupogen shots later, "it was finished!"

As a singer my entire life, I had only devoted the last eight years to gospel music. While I was going through radiation treatment, the doctors had advised me the radiation could affect my voice. It did not! I became more involved in singing than ever! All denominations opened their doors for me to visit, share my testimony, and sing. Being warned that I should not participate in a jail ministry due to my health and the exposure to illness, I continued to visit the jail and share the Word through music. The Lord protected me and I never even caught a slight cold during those many months. Throughout the entire treatment period, God continued to bless me with opportunities to sing and testify about His wondrous Love!

God allowed me to record my first CD in 2000, followed by two more recording projects. Today, God has blessed me with a full-time gospel music ministry, and I've been dubbed His "Christian Energizer Bunny"! I have been cancer-free for nearly eleven years, traveling all over the Midwest, sharing the love and promises of Christ Jesus! Twice chosen as one of Branson's favorite female gospel singers, I have been blessed by God with more in the Spirit than I could have ever dreamed! And He did it all… Thank You, Father!

A breast cancer survivor, Carol Sanguinette-How of Festus, Missouri, shares a testimony and love for God through her gospel music ministry. Twice chosen one of Branson's favorite female gospel singers, Carol is always ready to share!

God's on My Side

By Shirley Scarbrough

I am fifty-four years old and never graduated from high school. I have worked all my life, and the last thing I thought about was getting my G.E.D.

My job started getting slow, and I hurt my back and neck last year. I wasn't working very much, so I thought I would get my G.E.D. I took the package they gave me and went to G.E.D. classes. It was rough, since I had been out of school for forty years. I went to class for about eight months. I took the G.E.D. test and failed science, so I said I could do this. I took the science over again and didn't get a grade because they gave me the wrong test.

I prayed to God and said, "Lord, if it is Your will for me to get my G.E.D., then I will get it." I went and took the science part of it again and passed. I can tell anyone that if they have God on their side they can do anything. I owe Him my life for all He has done.

Shirley Scarbrough is currently unemployed and starting business classes in September. She was recently baptized. She currently resides in Jackson, Tennessee.

183

Surgery While Under God's Anesthesia

By Carolyn Scherer

It was in the early '80s when my father, who was a diabetic, had been having trouble with his feet and legs. My father pastored a small church in Grayville, Illinois, and had gotten to the point where he would have to sit down to preach. He was in pain most of the time.

He, of course, was seeing his doctor for this, and the doctor told him the nerves in his feet and legs were gone due to the diabetes. He lived on pain medicine, and the doctor told him the next step, when he was ready, would be amputation. This was very devastating to my family.

Several weeks later, we went to a special service in Granite City to see some friends of ours and to be in a "healing" service. Bro. Kenneth Reeves was a great instrument of the Lord when it came to praying for people. Toward the end of the service they asked for all those who needed a healing to come and be prayed for. My dad, of course, believed the Lord could heal him, but had been prayed for numerous times before and he thought the Lord was not ready to heal him. But with some urging from his friend, he went and got into the line, a very long line.

When it was his turn to be prayed for, Bro. Reeves laid hands on him. Within seconds, my dad was slain in the spirit; he was out cold. We, of course, were sitting in the congregation, praying and trying to believe while at the same being a little worried.

When he came to, we left and went home. This was on a Saturday night. My dad's pain persisted and was the worst it had ever been after that service. The next day, Sunday, was a very bad day for him. He could not even preach because the pain was so bad. But Monday morning he got up and drove his school bus route, and just like any other day went back home after getting the kids to school. As he was getting ready to eat breakfast, he kept thinking something was different, but he couldn't put his finger on it. He went to change his shoes and it suddenly dawned on him that he was not in pain. He did not hurt at all. The pain was gone! We testify that God performed surgery on him that night while he was slain.

Needless to say, we were rejoicing and praising God for His healing. My dad went back to the doctor and told him what had happened and that God had healed him. The doctor replied, "Well, I'm for anything that works." And we know God truly does work miracles. It's been more than twenty years, and my dad is still diabetic, but he still has his feet and legs.

Carolyn Scherer lives in Canton, Georgia, with her husband Ken, their son Nathan, and their daughter Megan.

A Miracle on Christmas Eve

By Wilma Shannon

It was late in the evening and I had been wrapping Christmas presents for my kids. My arm had been hurting for a couple of days and I thought it was from carrying shopping bags at the mall. The pain became so severe that I asked my husband, James, to take me to the emergency room at Ball Memorial Hospital.

Upon arrival, I was hurriedly rushed back to a room and hooked up to monitors. To my surprise, I was in the middle of a heart attack. I had never had any heart problems previously. I was blessed to have had one of the best cardiologists in the world, Dr. Chris Hollon, on duty when I was taken to the ER. My husband was told to call my family and tell them I probably wouldn't survive.

Hospital nurses asked my husband James, sons Shawn and Chris, and daughter-in-law Stacey, to exit the room while they were taking care of me. I remember thinking it would probably be the last time I would see my family on this earth. I began to cry as I could feel the life leaving my body. I looked up at Dr. Hollon and said, "Please help me; I don't want to die." I knew that if I did die, my heart was right with God, but I sure hated to leave my family. I have such a loving and caring family. I am blessed.

I was taken in for heart surgery, and they put in two stints. I stayed in the hospital several days. My family would not open their Christmas gifts or celebrate Christmas until I was home. When I finally got to go home, I only got to stay a few days until I was rushed back into heart surgery again, where they added four more stints.

That was four years ago. Today I am doing great. I still attend cardio rehab three to four times a week. I still travel with my family

(The Shannons) singing gospel music all across the nation. I try to get the word out to women everywhere that heart disease is the number one killer of women today. It is not just a man's disease any longer. I do not take any day for granted. I do not let the little things in life upset or bother me any longer. When you come that close to death, you realize what is important in life and what isn't.

The whole time that surgery was being done on me, I knew God was working through those surgeons' hands. I knew God was the greatest physician of all.

You read about all the miracles in the Bible, but God is still performing His miracles today. I am a living example.

Christmas Eve is a little more special to me now. I feel like God gave me a second chance at life. I will forever uplift His holy name in word and in song.

I truly believe angels are watching over me every day of my life. And when my time comes to cross over Jordan, I will have no regrets because through God I have been blessed.

Wilma Shannon lives in Muncie, Indiana. She sings in a southern gospel group, The Shannons, which is comprised of her husband James, sons Shawn and Chris, and daughter-in-law Stacey. She has also published seven cookbooks to date.

My Song

By Doris Sherman

My day was going terribly. As I was driving to the hospital, I began to wonder if life would ever be sane again. My dad had recently been diagnosed with lung cancer. My siblings all lived away, and I bore the load of caring for my elderly folks. This new problem meant I would have to drive my dad sixty miles daily for six weeks to the nearest facility for radiation. We had three young sons that kept me busy, and my husband worked shift work and was away a lot. His sisters also lived away and he, being the baby of the family, assumed the responsibility of his mom—or rather, we both did.

She was now gone, a good, hardworking woman. My mother-in-law and her husband had died the year before. They had been involved in a car accident they never really recovered from. Walter died first, several months after the accident and his cardiac arrest. His body was just too worn out to take anymore. Geneva, who recuperated from a head wound, never recovered from a broken heart. Walter was her third husband death had claimed. Cruel fate.

Our oldest son had been seriously ill and I was getting worn out. I began to feel like Job, only without the taunting friends. My husband, while a good man, didn't know the Lord. Like many women, I thought marriage would change him. I was wrong. I couldn't talk to him even if I wanted to because he was feeling overwhelmed from the past few months and I didn't want to worry him further. I was trying to be strong for everyone, but I felt like I was drowning and going down for the third time. I was hurting and carried a heavy load. I couldn't even talk to my mom—she was already distraught—but while trying to keep a strong appearance for everyone, I felt so alone. The weight of the world was dragging me down.

I started talking to the Lord as I often did, but this time it was different. I was desperate, and the thought that was to become a song, my song, came to me: "It's me again, Lord. Don't You get tired of me always coming to You?" I asked Him. "But Lord, I don't know where else to turn. I need You, as the tears run down my face."

Somewhere during the next few miles God gave me a song, and not only a song, but also reassurance and peace. I knew that even though I didn't feel I had anyone else to talk to, I really did. I had Him, and He was enough.

Many years later, I still sing that song. It's as dear to me today as the day He gave it to me. These are the words to the chorus He gave me: "It's You and me together, Lord, again. And with Your help I'll see this through; I know I can. Please lift my burden higher, Lord, and let me lean on Thee. It's in Your never-failing love, Your mercies, Lord, I see."

Doris Sherman is married, the mother of three sons, and a grandmother of six residing in Houlton, Maine. She has belonged to the same little Baptist church for more than forty years, where she plays the piano and sings southern gospel music. She is also an emergency room nurse.

Ain't God Good?

Rev. Bobby L. Simmons

My grandson, Blake Spivey, was diagnosed in April of 2006 with Lymphoblastic Leukemia with the Philadelphia Syndrome. He was just four years old, and to say we were devastated would be an understatement. We were told they could get him to remission but that without a stem cell transplant he would almost one hundred percent relapse due to the Philadelphia Syndrome.

After a month of chemo and hospital stays, his blood was sent to Fairview Children's Hospital at the University of Minnesota. The results came back—he did need a stem cell transplant, but the Philadelphia Chromosome was not there. This was an impossibility with medicine. But not with God. That chromosome has never been found again. A stem cell match is not an easy thing, and the odds of finding a perfect match are astronomical. We found three. Ain't God good?

After four months in the hospital and the Ronald McDonald House in Minneapolis, Minnesota, Blake was able to return home. We celebrated one year of his being cancer-free in June, and in July we are celebrating the anniversary of his transplant.

I have been pastoring for almost seventeen years and I know God's awesome power, but I must admit all I have done this past year is said, "Wow!"

Things I have been promised in His precious Word and should expect simply continue to amaze this preacher. It is easy to tell others to have faith, but when you need to exercise it yourself, it sometimes seems much harder. Prayer and faith still work; just try it.

Rev. Bobby L. Simmons is pastor of Faith Baptist Church in College Park, Georgia. In 1979 he accepted the call to preach and has been pastoring since 1991.

The Blood of Jesus

By Candice Smith

I had a breakdown several years ago. I cannot describe it completely, but I felt like I was dying. The life literally felt like it was leaving my body, and I was overcome by this tremendous fear that was taking over my life.

After many ER visits to check my heart, they said it was panic attacks. I felt helpless. I was saved. How could this happen to a Christian? An ER nurse witnessed to me about the limits she had, but she reminded me of the unlimited power of God. Doctors told me there was no cure, only pills and treatment.

After months of Xanax, Paxil, Prozac, and other medications I cannot remember, I decided to press in even more to God. I could not sleep for days until my body would shut down. There were times a shot was required to calm me down. I cried all the time without knowing why. I could not function. What would happen to my son and husband? I went for months without working. I kept reaching for God. Then it happened. After many services and prayer lines, I was filled with the Holy Ghost.

I began to recover slowly. Time with God was my medicine. Hours of Bible study and praying were all I had to relieve me. The pharmacy did not have my miracle. Regardless of the reports, I flushed the nerve pills and have been free for more than seven years. It was a battle and there were days it tried to come back, but my Lord is all I need. The blood of Jesus healed me, and I am still whole today! Praise the Lord!

Candice Smith is thirty-six years old. She ministers a small radio broadcast twice a month, and she sings and ministers in church while also working a full-time job.

The Prayer

By Gregg Smith

During the Independence Day weekend of 2006, I was the emcee for a gospel sing at Riverfest in St. Albans, West Virginia. I had been doing other radio work for a few years, but this was my first opportunity to emcee a gospel concert in a few years, and the rust showed. I failed to adequately prepare in advance and wound up ad-libbing and saying whatever came to mind as I introduced each artist. By the time the final group was ready to appear, I was so nervous I really couldn't think straight, but I had to face the fear and make the best introduction I could.

That group just happened to be Jeff and Sheri Easter. Because I was not prepared, I actually ran out of things to say as I kept the large crowd engaged while Jeff and Sheri got set up on stage. I thought to myself, "I'll just talk about how many number one hits they've had." After I started the sentence, I realized I didn't know how many number one hits they actually had, but being such a popular group with so many hits, I didn't think it would be possible they hadn't had any *Singing News* number one songs. I just turned to Jeff, who was standing on stage near me, and said, "How many number one hits have you had?"

Being the professional that Jeff is, he just replied without missing a beat, "Bunches!" Somehow I got us out of that mess and introduced them, and they played a very inspired set of music.

That night, as I was lying down to go to sleep, I reflected on the evening. I just got this overwhelming feeling the actual answer to that question was "none." They really had never had a number one hit in the *Singing News*. Who can blame Jeff for his response, being put on the spot like that? What was he supposed to say—"None"?

I remember vividly what happened next. I prayed, "Father, I am so sorry I was not well prepared. Please forgive me. I will prepare in advance next time. Father, could You please bless Jeff and Sheri Easter, and send 'Over and Over' to number one? I promise I will testify and bring glory to Your name because of it."

A few months later, I saw a headline in one of my radio updates, Stating, "Jeff and Sheri Easter's 'Over and Over' becomes their first ever number one hit in the *Singing News*." I immediately knew in my heart that God had answered my prayer. Jeff and Sheri have had many awesome songs. It's no coincidence that "Over and Over" was the first one to reach the top of the *Singing News* Chart.

I saw Jeff a few months ago and told him this story. And now God has given me the opportunity to share it with all of you reading this. I thank God for the answered prayer and the opportunity to testify to so many people. Praise the Lord!

Gregg Smith is a traffic reporter during the week for six radio stations and one television station in Charleston, West Virginia. On Sundays, he hosts a gospel music program called "The Sunday Gospel Sunrise," and plays drums in the praise band at Oakwood Baptist Church.

God Is so Good

By Rita S. Spivey

There were two specific low times in my life when God blessed me and my family. The first blessing was actually before my struggle hit in the fall of 1999. God knew I was going to be facing a diagnosis, surgery, and treatment of breast cancer over the next eight months, not to mention the challenge of taking care of my two small children and husband and working a full-time job during that time. Just prior to that situation, I had heard on the Gospel Greats that the Inspirations were hosting a contest to win a nine-day stay in Bryson City and tickets to attend their singing event that summer. After submitting a postcard, I received a call from Paul Heil that I had won. What a wonderful and relaxing time we had in Bryson City. I think it was just what the doctor ordered!

The second blessing came in 2002 after a very hard six months of helping to take care of my mother, who was dying of cancer. After her passing, my family needed some down time to get away on a much-needed vacation, but just didn't have the extra money to do so. God blessed us again with winning a small sweepstakes that allowed our family to go on a seven-day vacation at the beach. The strange thing was that my husband did not even remember registering us for that sweepstakes. What a mighty and caring God we serve!

Rita S. Spivey lives in the Hickory, North Carolina, area. She has been a church secretary at Waldensian Presbyterian Church in Valdese, North Carolina, for eleven years. She enjoys reading; going shopping with her thirteen-year-old daughter, Brooklyn; visiting with her twenty-year-old son, Jordan, at college; and traveling with her husband, David. The family attends Mountain View Baptist Church in Hickory.

The Healing Touch

By Dr. Garry L. Spriggs

In the '40s, I was a puny kid. I always had allergies, and during fall my hay fever would kick in and make me and everyone else around me miserable. I would go visit my aunt's farm to play with my cousins during the summer months, but I couldn't survive the ragweed. My eyes were swollen and my nose was either running or stopped up so badly I couldn't breathe. Most of my time was spent indoors. Even with no air conditioning it provided some relief.

I would also get a fever at the drop of a hat. In those days doctors didn't know much to do for me. They told my mom I was close to having rheumatic fever when I was very young. My mom would put cold washcloths on my forehead and give me aspirin. I remember many cold baths as she tried to bring my fever below 103-104. It would spike up quickly and worry her. I was a mess.

I clearly remember one night when I was eight years old that my fever hit the dangerous 104 mark. It was about 2 a.m. when mom knelt by my bed and poured her heart out to God on my behalf. There were no thoughts of going to the emergency room; people didn't do that when I was eight. She also knew the family doctor had no answers, so why wake him up?

She went to the kitchen and got some olive oil and proceeded to anoint me and pray. While she was praying, my fever broke and I began to sweat profusely. I literally soaked the bed as my fever returned to normal. It all happened within a half hour. God had heard my mom; she was good at that!

The fact that my fever broke that night is only part of the miracle. That incident took place sixty years ago, and if you were to take my temperature right now, it would be almost a full degree below normal. I have been sick many times since then, but if I get a fever today of 99, it means I am really sick. I have never had the extreme fevers again, and only on rare occasions has it been above 99 or 100. It was a miracle.

Though the house has long been torn down where that eventful night took place, I try to make an annual trek by the vacant corner and remember vividly how the supreme Creator of the universe came down to answer my mother's prayer on my behalf. I wasn't much in this world's value system, but in God's economy, I was worth a personal visit!

Can all this be considered coincidental? I think not. It was beyond mere coincidence. It was God!

Dr. Garry L. Spriggs is an ordained minister residing in Akron, Ohio. Dr. Spriggs has been in ministry since 1961, when he took his first pastorate. In addition to being a pastor, he has been an evangelist and Bible college administrator. He is also a published author.

My Heart in His Hands

By Mary Jane Stanley

Little did I know how God was looking out for me on February 28, 2007. It was a Wednesday night, and my husband and I had not attended church because I was having what I thought were muscle spasms. As a general rule I do not take aspirin, but this night I did. Things eased and I went to sleep.

On Saturday, March 3, the spasms were back, but with a difference. I became nauseated, broke out in a cold sweat, and my heart was racing. You guessed it—symptoms of a heart attack.

I spent the night in the hospital; praise God, it was not a heart attack, only a warning. To make a long story short, I had a heart cath on March 9 and was told I would have to undergo bypass surgery. The surgeon would not send me home because I had three critical blockages. He told me that if I demanded to go home I could, but if anything happened it would be on me, not him. He also said he could keep me laying around the hospital with a nitro-drip and hope nothing happened for three or four days, or he could get the people in there Saturday morning, the next day, to do the job. I chose the next day. He later told my husband that someone could have cut me off while driving and scared me and I could have had a massive heart attack.

God had His hand around my heart. He kept my heart going when I so easily could have had a massive heart attack. I know He has a reason for me to be here, and I know He will show me what He wants me to do. Until then I will continue to praise Him and tell anyone who will listen that only by the grace of God am I still here!

Raised in the hills of Southern Ohio, Mary Jane Stanley moved to the South in 1982. She currently resides in Mississippi.

God's Little Miracle

By Tony Stewart

My wife and I decided we would like to have a child after three years of marriage. My wife was diagnosed with polycystic ovarian disease and was not a good candidate for getting pregnant. We prayed for a child at home, in prayer meetings, and everywhere for a year. Then God sent us to a Christian doctor who put her on different medicines to help us to conceive. They did not work, so we decided to try artificial insemination. That failed, too. We then decided to adopt a child if we were not going to have one ourselves. We went to classes for three months, then found out that because of my past police record, we were not eligible to adopt.

After a year and six months, we told God we were through trying to have a child. We still had a desire for a child, but we came to accept the fact we were not going to have one. The doctors had told us we were not going to be able to conceive, even after my wife had surgery to try to clear up her disease, and we were not financially able to keeping trying all the different medical methods. But we never gave up on God.

Ten months and hundreds of prayers later, we found out that God had kept His Word. In April of 2002, we found out we were going to have a child. We promised God we would raise this child in a Christian home, and He kept His promise to us.

My son, Logan Matthew Stewart, is now five years old and starting kindergarten this year. He loves to get on stage at church and sing God's praises. He is a wonderful little miracle from God. God likes to work when nothing else will. Praise God for all He's done and for all He is going to do!

Tony Stewart is a 42-year-old father of three children, Jessica, Tony Jr., and Logan. He is married to Cheryl, and they live in Jackson, Tennessee. He sings and plays drums, teaches Sunday school, and is a former youth leader at Parkway Church of God.

It's a Miracle!

By Rev. Allan Stokes, Sr.

February 6, 2007. The day will forever be etched in my mind. For some there was 9/11, but for me there was 2/6/07.

The day started out as planned. Our daughter Sarah was to check in to the hospital for the birth of our second grandson. The labor was slow, and besides a few adverse reactions by the baby to medications, uneventful.

Soon after he was born, the atmosphere in the room changed. Without explanation, he was whisked out of the delivery room and transferred to NICU. "His blood sugar is extremely low," one nurse mumbled as she rushed out the door. Later, doctors explained that Joshua had a small brain bleed. Soon after he began to have seizures, an external sign that something was going on inside his tiny body.

Several days later, doctors determined that the "bleed" was in fact a blood clot in the front of the brain. I will never forget the utter grief I felt when the doctor said, "Your baby has suffered a stroke, and there is some brain damage. At his point we don't know how much, or what area."

Doctors ordered us not to pick him up, rub him, or stimulate him in any way, for fear of inducing more seizures. We were allowed to sit by his crib during visits. I laid my hand on his little body and spoke to his blood, "I demand you to flow in the name of Jesus."

Doctors wanted to move him to Louisville, Kentucky, but we felt led to Vanderbilt Children's Hospital in Nashville, Tennessee. The doctors conceded, and our request was granted, our prayers were answered. The original plan was to fly him out, but due to adverse weather, that plan was scrapped. My son, a paramedic with the local ambulance service, received authorization to take the trip. Another prayer was answered.

En route to Nashville, we called every number that was programmed in our cell phone's memory and asked for prayer. We begged our family and friends to call everyone they knew and "believe God for a miracle for Joshua Lee."

When we arrived in Nashville, we were bombarded with a team of specialists, including a pediatric neurologist and a pediatric hematologist. Every conceivable test was run. Every option was explored. Our days hinged on the doctors' next visits. We knew when to expect the next "team" to come in. Calls came in from across the United States. E-mails filled our inboxes, promises of prayers for a "miracle for Joshua Lee."

Finally, after the doctors were convinced they had all the results back, we were told we could take Joshua home. With very little fanfare, we were dismissed and made the two-hour trip back home. Hours turned to days, days to weeks, and weeks to months.

During a return trip to the pediatric neurologist, while looking over the records, he nonchalantly grunted, "Humm." He looked at Joshua Lee, back at the computer screen, and then concluded, "I can see the obvious blood clot on the MRIs from the previous hospital, but in the entire series of tests we took, we were never able to find a clot." And then he finished by saying, "No doubt it was there, but somewhere between Madisonville and Nashville, it disappeared."

Tears flowed freely down my face as I replied, "That is amazing, but not surprising."

Joshua Lee was healed by the very hand of God. Praise God! Today he is a living testimony that miracles still happen. We share his testimony everywhere we go, with anyone who will listen.

Rev. Allan Stokes, Sr., resides in Madisonville, Kentucky. He and his wife, Joy Lynne, have been married twenty-nine years. They have three children and three grandsons, and they are expecting their fourth grandchild in April 2008. He is senior pastor of Pleasant Hill Pentecostal Church in Cadiz.

Recurring Dream

By Lanny Swaim

When I was eleven or twelve years old I had a recurring dream every night for weeks. In this dream I was always playing with little plastic horses in the dirt in a neighbor's backyard. In every dream I was with a little girl about my age. She was cute but her face was always a little dirty; I suppose it was because we were playing in the dirt. It was winter and she always wore a gray coat that was little, tattered, and torn. This little girl was my best friend, and I knew that one day we would grow up and get married.

I did grow up, and my first marriage lasted ten years. My first wife left me when my sons were six and eight years old. I later gained custody of both boys. I remarried three years after my first marriage ended. Cathy and I have now been married for twenty-one years. After we married, she adopted my sons.

Those first years of marriage to Cathy were difficult. We had a wonderful relationship, but raising my two teenage sons and her teenage daughter in a blended family proved to be a challenge. At one point, I began to wonder if I had made a mistake by remarrying with two young sons.

Cathy had almost no pictures of herself or her family when she was a child. Her parents had split up when she was young and most of her childhood pictures had been lost. One day she found two 5x7 pictures she had put away. One was of her as a little girl and the other was her older brother, Michael. She dusted them off and displayed them in our living room.

When I looked at the picture of Cathy as a little girl, I suddenly remembered the recurring dream I had as a young boy. The picture I was looking at was the girl in the dream. When I told Cathy this story she gave me a look of unbelief at first. But when I got to the part about playing with little plastic horses in the dirt in someone's backyard, tears came into her eyes.

She told me she used to save her allowance and take it to town with her on Saturday mornings. Richardson's Department Store was on Main Street in High Point, North Carolina, where we both grew up. In the front of Richardson's were two big wooden tables with all kinds of toys and trinkets on them. Everything on those tables sold for a penny each. Cathy would buy little plastic horses, take them home, and play with them in the dirt in her backyard.

I have never since doubted that God brought us together and that our marriage was planned long before either of us was born.

Did God cause my first marriage or Cathy's first marriage to fail? Definitely not! Malachi 2:16 says that God hates divorce. But my loving heavenly Father knew the path our lives would take, and at the proper time he caused those paths to cross.

Today, when I think of that recurring dream, it seems so real. It is almost as if Cathy and I have a history that started long before we met. Perhaps we do.

Lanny Swaim has led praise and worship in church settings and with various ministries in the US and Europe. As a teacher, prophet, psalmist, praise and worship leader, and southern gospel recording artist, he is frequently invited to minister in churches, conferences, etc.

One Ordinary Night

By Bruce Taylor

While I was driving along, I was beginning to get tired. Rightly so, because I had been driving for thirty hours and I still had six hours to go. Then my headlights came upon someone alongside the road.

As I got closer, I saw it was just a hitchhiker. Needing someone to talk to, I decided to stop. We continued on and started to talk. Right away He knew I was too tired to be driving. He gladly offered to drive for me, but I was reluctant. He kept offering to drive, but I wasn't sure He could handle my big truck. On His fourth attempt, I agreed. When I awoke, we were safely at our destination. But there was one thing I could not understand. Just as I was dozing off, I heard the voice on the C.B. say, "Look at that truck! The driver is in the jump seat! But there is no one driving!"

"Was I dreaming?" I asked my newfound friend.

"Yes, I heard it," He said.

"But I don't understand," I replied.

He answered, "The reason they did not see Me is because they do not know Me. You can see Me because you stopped and invited Me into your truck. I am your new partner. Whenever you are tired, I will let you rest. Whenever you must unload your load, I will be your lumper."

Now we really make the miles, my friend and I. I never get tired because He is always there when I need him. He shares all the good things with me. I introduce Him to all my friends. If you don't know Him, I would like to introduce Him to you. His name is Jesus. He is the best friend you can have. You can meet Him if you allow Him to come into your heart. You won't be sorry. Take it from me. I never regretted stopping to take time to let him in.

Matthew 11:28 says, "Come to me and I will give you rest." Jesus said these words.

Truckers are tired people because they work such long, hard hours. You need rest, but you need to ask for it. The words say, "Come unto me and I(Jesus)will give you rest." It requires that you come first. Then you can receive the rest.

Bruce Taylor is married to Sandy and has been driving a truck for twenty-five years. He has been saved for nineteen years and has recently answered God's call to preach.

The Miracle of Life

By Doris TenElshof

He didn't have the strength to put on his socks! My husband, a tall, strong man sat quietly in his recliner. He had been feeling tired for a few weeks, but the feelings of extreme weakness were a frightening new symptom. I helped him with his socks and shoes and drove him to the office of our family physician. Dr. Switzer, a trusted and gifted doctor as well as a treasured friend, welcomed us into his personal office, where he asked many questions regarding Ken's symptoms. He then directed my husband to an examination room and quietly nodded for me to wait outside the room. It was then he told me, "I am sorry to tell you this, but all indications are that you should prepare yourself. I feel Ken is gravely ill. I want you to be prepared."

Ken was admitted to the hospital, and the tests and biopsies were ongoing for nearly three weeks. It was during this time we were surrounded by people who prayed with us and for us. Although extremely weak, Ken never seemed to lose his strength of spirit. He never gave up and thanked God for each day. The prayers lifted up for him were giving him the will to remain positive…he wanted to live!

At the foot of his bed was a chalkboard on which was written the name of the charge nurse for each shift. Each day I added a Bible verse to the board and he would quietly look to it for comfort and encouragement. Even nurses and doctors began checking to see the "verse of the day."

During this time we held tightly to the prayers and Bible verses, and each day we prayed his life would be spared—we dared to pray for a miracle. After three weeks the decision was made to perform surgery. The doctors expected the worst and instead found a miracle!

The dreaded form of cancer was totally encapsulated, and no chemo-therapy or radiation treatments were needed!

Five years have passed, and each day we are aware of our personal "miracle." We never cease to praise a loving and gracious God...one who answered prayers.

My husband's favorite Bible verse written on the chalkboard at the foot of his bed was "Be still and know that I am God." We were "still," waiting to know God's will, and His will was for an extended life. We are filled with thankfulness and praise—for family and friends who were faithful, for doctors who were not ashamed to ask for God's guid-ance, and most of all for a loving Father. What a cause for praise!

Doris TenElshof was born and raised in a small town in Minnesota and has since lived in North Carolina, Kansas, and Michigan. Although semi-retired, she works part-time in a funeral home.

Forever Healed

By Ben Thompson

On July 8, 1966, I had a serious back injury at work. The pain was so severe that I passed out at around 8:10 a.m. The next thing I knew, I was in the hospital in traction and it was 4:30 p.m.

After that, I was off work for eight months. The pain was gone, but three or four times it returned to my back, then to my hip, then to my left ankle. I had to walk on crutches for two or three weeks, and then it went away.

Eight years later in 1974, I was in a regular Wednesday night service on my crutches. At the end of the service, the pastor asked for anyone who wanted healing to come to the altar. I stepped out in the aisle, and before I took my first step forward, I was forever healed. Thirty-three years later, I am still healed. Praise His holy name.

Ben Thompson is sixty-seven years old and married to Vivian. He retired in 2003 and now makes his home in Somerset, Kentucky.

God Is Good All the Time

By Elizabeth Trent

My husband Gary and I have been married for almost seven years. God chose to bless us with a beautiful daughter, Emily Brooke Trent, on January 1, 2005. She was our firstborn. At the age of three months she was diagnosed with dilated cardiomyopathy (an enlarged heart). She stayed in the hospital for three weeks and was placed on seven medications. She had a couple of other short hospital stays to try a new medication. She was admitted once again on October 14, 2005, due to needing oxygen.

She was placed on Medos (a heart assist device) on October 28, 2005, after the PICU staff tried to put a breathing tube in. Her heart stopped for forty-seven minutes and her brain began to bleed and swell. After a couple weeks of being on the Medos, we decided to take Emily off due to risk of blood clots. On November 10, 2005, she was taken into surgery to have the Medos taken out. While transferring her from the operating table to her hospital bed after surgery, she went into cardiac arrest and never recovered. She passed away that day at the tender age of ten months and nine days. Though it was very difficult to let her go, we know she is no longer suffering or in pain. She has a perfect heart now and is God's sweet little angel who watches over us daily.

God is faithful if you just cling to Him and trust Him for every detail of your life.

Six months later, we were blessed with the joyous news of another pregnancy. Our son, Stewart Wayne Trent, was born December 11, 2006. He is a precious gift from heaven and our beautiful miracle.

Praise the Lord! God is good all the time. All the time God is good.

Elizabeth Trent has been married to her husband, Gary, since September 30, 2000. They live in Tucson, Arizona.

God's Not Finished With Me Yet!

By Jerry Trent

In January 1980 I had a heart attack. It isn't a big deal until you realize I was only thirty-seven years old. In March of the same year I had open heart surgery and five bypasses again—no big deal. God pulled me through. I was singing gospel at the time, and was a bass in the gospel quartet.

This went on until 1990 when I had to have open heart surgery again. I had four bypasses this time and then another heart attack. I was forty-seven at this time.

In July 1999 I had another heart attack, this time when I was seventy miles from home, so I drove to the hospital in Oklahoma City by myself. In 1999 my excellent cardiologist gave me three stents. In October of that year I had three more stents inserted. This time it was because I was still having chest pains.

In January 2005 I was still having chest pains, so I went in for another stent. This time, instead of having a stent inserted, the doctor tried to straighten one out that had turned crossways. I had a stroke. I was rushed over to Mercy Health Center, where at least two doctors worked a total of nine hours on me to get me through the stroke. I was in physical therapy for four weeks while I stayed in the hospital.

I now drive a van for a company which hauls students to a school and takes them back home at night.

I praise God for His mercy with me and for giving the physicians the knowledge to know what to do next.

Jerry Trent is sixty-five years old and has been a Christian for about forty years. He is married and has two sons living in North Carolina, a stepson in Dallas, and a stepson and stepdaughter in Oklahoma City. He has nine grandchildren.

Your Loved One Is Home

By Wayne Trexler

My oldest son was killed in an auto accident April 30, 2007. He was thirty-four and was going to be married in September. This is what happened and how God, through little things and a song, let us know he was home.

I received the phone call from a passerby, and not the police. He got the number off the truck. He called and said one of my trucks was in a bad wreck.

I said, "Is he all right?"

He said, "He did not make it."

My wife was sitting right in front of me. I didn't know what to say.

I can hardly remember driving up there. I called my other son, and he was on his way. He told me later he was praying over and over again that Scott was not dead. Then he said he heard a soft voice say, "He is with me. He is with me," and he knew he was gone.

When we got to the wreck, they would not let us go near it. The person who called me came over and said he was sorry and he did not know it was my son. He then asked if he was a Christian.

I said, "Yes, he was."

He said, "I thought so, because I had seen some flyers in his truck for a gospel singing he was putting on."

The day before the funeral, I put on the watch he had been wearing. I didn't like to wear a watch, but I wanted to wear his. That watch alarm went off at 5:00 every morning for three days in a row. Scott was never a morning person, and I knew he didn't have it set for that time.

The next thing that happened was my grandson, who was three, was in bed in between his mom and dad that night. They were just about to fall asleep when they herd something in the kitchen. It was the dishwasher. Jaxon sat up in between them and said, "Scott's been in a wreck and he's in heaven." It was like someone had told him to say it.

At his funeral we played the song "Got Here as Fast as I Could" by Mark Bishop. Scott really liked that song. About three days after the funeral some friends told me they had not heard the ad on the radio for the gospel sing, so I called the station and got put on hold. Guess what was playing in the background? "Got Here as Fast as I Could."

That same day I went back to work. At about the same time that Scott's wreck took place, there was a wreck right in front of our business. The wreck was about the same kind that Scott had been in. My wife and I were the first ones to get there, and you know what we had on our minds. The lady had to be taken to the hospital, but all she could say was that she was so sorry for our loss. After they took her away, we walked back to work. Guess what was playing on the radio? "Got Here as Fast as I Could."

I do not believe these are coincidences. I believe this was God letting us know our son was home with Him and waiting for us with his arms open wide.

Wayne Trexler and his wife Robin currently reside in Rockwell, North Carolina. They have been married for thirty-seven years.

The Return Visit

By Alma Kay Turk

In late spring I felt a large lump in the middle of my body underneath my rib cage. I went to our family doctor, who called it a hernia and referred me to a surgeon. The surgeon ordered a CT scan with an appointment to follow-up the next week. I kept praying it would go away and I wouldn't need surgery.

The surgeon felt this lump also. Well, on my return visit to him he came in with great news. Whatever it was had left and gone away with God's healing hands on my body. Only He could do that with the power of prayer. I was just so very thankful to Him that I wouldn't have to face the knife again. And nothing showed up in the CT scan either.

Alma Kay Turk is a 66-year-old wife, mother, and grandmother. She lives in Owosso, Michigan, with her husband, Art, and their two youngest sons.

For Sale

By Deborah Twiford

My husband and I were stationed in Montgomery, Alabama, for six years. While living there, I watched some of my husband's co-workers get transferred to distant places. The husband would have to go on to the new duty station and leave the wife and children behind to keep the house clean and the yard mowed until the house sold. Sometimes that took two years! I always hated being separated from my husband while he went on business trips for a few weeks at a time, so the thought of a possible two-year separation was unbearable. Rather than worry about it, I began to pray daily that God would not let that happen to us.

One Tuesday while at work, my next door neighbor, a realtor, called me. He said, "Deb, I've been showing houses to this couple for three days and they don't like anything I've shown them. I finally just pulled the car over and asked them to describe their dream house, and they described your house to a tee. Would it be okay with you if I came up to your office and got the key to your house and showed them your house?"

I agreed, and he showed them our house. When we got home from work, there was a contract for the sale of our house on our dining room table. Three days later we found out my husband's bosses were flying in to the airport on Sunday and he was to pick them up at the airport. As they got off the plane, they notified my husband that we were being transferred to Dallas. We had already sold our house there. I called our neighbor, the realtor, to let him know. He immediately came over and put a For Sale sign in our front yard. We got two more contracts for the purchase of our house in that week. That was an answered prayer if there ever was one! I still thank God for that one regularly!

Deborah Twiford lives in the country North of Goldthwaite, Texas, with her husband, David, to whom she has been married for forty years. They work together in a funeral home in Brownwood.

The Fence—Before, Behind and Beyond

By Helen VanScyoc

I was raised in church all my life. My dad died when I was seventeen, and when I graduated, I wandered away from God—much like the prodigal son.

Over the next seventeen years, I fell into deep sin. I went through a divorce when my husband had an affair with my best friend. I became entangled in a life of alcohol, drugs, and men, and at one point, I had even tried to kill myself. A few weeks later I became involved with a married man, and for the next four years, I was caught in that lifestyle.

Where would it all end?

I became friends with a saintly old lady who looked beyond the bad in me and saw the potential. She invited me to her church. God's love began to melt through all the muddle in my life and I turned my heart toward home, toward God, who was standing there—much like the father of the prodigal son.

I made my peace with God and married a wonderful Christian man. And then the bottom fell out of my life once again. Being in dire financial trouble (or at least what seemed dire to me), I stole some money from my employer; not a lot, just 533 dollars. Although it wasn't a lot, my boss pressed charges for petty theft. Having had a previous record for writing bad checks, I was facing a felony charge.

Long story short, I entered a guilty plea to the charges and was convicted and sentenced to one year in jail. Not just any jail, but the

Ohio Women's Reformatory. Not just any day, but three days before Christmas.

As I entered that horrible place, questions flooded my mind: would my husband leave me? How would I ever survive in such a place for the next twelve months?

I did a lot of soul searching. I had asked God to forgive me for my sins, and He had. I even asked the man I had wronged for his forgiveness, but he didn't forgive me.

Over the next seven weeks, I realized God's Word was true when it said, "you reap what you sow." But in spite of it all, God was with me and used my life to witness for Him.

Then the day came I was to go to a shock probation hearing. Seven weeks after entering the big iron gate, I was on my way out of there. "Gloria," who had badgered me the whole time I was there because of my stand for Christ, came running to me as I was leaving. I said to her, "Look, you've given me nothing but trouble ever since I've been in here. I'm on my way out the door; you are not going to do anything to cause me trouble and keep me from being able to leave and go home to my family."

Gloria then said, "Look, I know I've given you a lot of trouble. But I just wanted you to know that if I ever become a Christian, it will be because I saw Christ in you." We hugged each other and went our separate ways—I to freedom and Gloria to remain in prison.

I can't tell you where "Gloria" is today, but I can tell you this story is a testimony of God's faithfulness—even in the most desolate circumstances. Would I want to do it again? No! But I am thankful for the experience I gleaned from it. In the words of Karen Peck's song, "God is faithful"!

Helen VanScyoc of Mount Vernon, Ohio, travels and sings with The Singing Smiths of Pataskala, and shares her testimony whenever God opens the door.

A Miracle-Working God

By Audrey Vigliotto

My brother was diagnosed with kidney disease. A 4.0 dialysis had to begin, otherwise he would have ten days to two weeks to live. All his kids and friends were called in to say goodbye when the reading reached 3.9. Tests were done every two weeks so pain medication, home healthcare, etc. would make the end as painless as possible. Relatives and church groups across the U.S. were called to pray for Cleve St. Clair. They all prayed, "God, just make his end easy."

After a two-week wait and more blood work, the results were 3.2. The nurse said, "Don't get too excited"—whatever that meant. Two weeks later, the nurse called to say, "We don't understand; we can't explain it, but the result is 2.6."

We can explain! God is still working miracles. As great as this story is, there's a better one: On Sunday morning during praise time, Cleve stood to his feet in the choir and said, "If you've not heard, God has healed my kidneys. So you don't need to drop by the house anymore to pick up things I'm giving away. I'm not dying. Well, you can drop by and return the stuff I've already given you."

It's hard to say which was the loudest: "Hallelujah!" or "Praise the Lord!" or the laughter that arose as this proper, dignified, professional man told his brothers and sisters in Christ God was still working miracles.

Audrey Vigliotto began singing southern gospel music with a mixed quartet when she was fifteen. As of today, she is still singing Southern gospel. She also leads a choir, teaches a Sunday school class, and heads up a singles' group in a Southern Baptist church.

Peace That Passeth Understanding

By Wilma Jean Whitlatch

God knew how difficult it was for me to live so far from my elderly parents. I wished to be nearby to help with the challenges they faced.

In March, I told my husband Alan I needed to make another trip to visit my mother in Tampa, Florida. Alan said he could take me Easter weekend.

A few hours after our arrival on Friday, we were informed Mom did not have long to live. I wasn't expecting that news.

Later that day, one of the caregivers stopped me in the hall to tell me she had heard Mom pray. She said it brought back childhood memories of going to church and learning about Jesus. God still had a purpose for Mom's life. My mother could still pray, and she remembered hymns and choruses until the last few months of her life.

After spending most of the night, I decided to get a little rest and attend an early Easter service. The message that morning was about Christ being the center of our lives. After the service, I went back to the nursing home with Alan and my brother. I quoted Psalms 23 and sang a song to Mom she had taught our family.

A nurse stepped in the room. She commented that I needed to release Mom to God's mercy. After she left the room, I turned around to try and pull a chair up next to the bed. When I turned back around, Mom's eyes were the prettiest blue-gray I had seen. I couldn't help but wonder if Mom was seeing heaven. I put my head next to her head and prayed for Jesus to come and lead Mom home to heaven. Within five minutes, Mom went home to be with her Savior in heaven. I believe Jesus did come and lead her home.

God knew how important it was for me to be with Mom that day, and He orchestrated everything so I could be there. What a time for Mom to enter heaven—Easter Sunday!

My father passed away in January 2001. God provided for me to be with my dad then. Dad's roommate rolled his wheelchair up by my side as I stood by Dad's bed. He requested I ask my Dad if he would tell his mother he was going to see her in heaven someday. I turned to my dad and asked if he knew Jesus as his Savior. He indicated that he did. Then I said, "Dad, when you see Lela May Williams would you tell her that her son, Don Williams, will see her in heaven?" I started singing "Amazing Grace," and Dad went home to heaven. A peace filled that room.

The morning of Dad's funeral, I picked up my Bible. God had been faithful to give me comfort and assurance and speak to me through His Word. I wondered if He would have something for me then. My Bible fell open to Psalm 116:15.

Mom and Dad taught me about God's love. As a child, I bowed at an altar of prayer. I knew there was sin in my life because God's Word says "all have sinned." I believed Jesus was born of a virgin and died on a cross so I could be saved from my sins. I knew many Easters ago that He rose from the dead.

That spring Sunday, after I'd asked Jesus into my life, I felt free from the burden of sin. Because of God's forgiveness, I know I will see Jesus and will also one day see my mother and father in heaven.

Wilma Jean Whitlatch is a devoted wife and mother of two daughters. She and her husband, Alan, have three grandchildren. She has worked outside of the home as a secretary and administrative assistant for more than thirty years. She and her husband reside in Greer, South Carolina.

My Boss, My Guardian Angel!

By Karen L. Williamson

One Monday morning at work I had a severe pain in my chest and down my left arm. Since I was there by myself I knew what I had to do. I called to God and said, "It is just You and me here? Please take care of me." And God did just that! I was able to stay at work for a while longer until my boss (my guardian angel) realized something was wrong. My boss kept trying to get me to go to the doctor, but I wouldn't go. He got a co-worker to take me to my cardiologist, where he ran an EKG and told me I was going straight to the hospital.

I said, "My husband doesn't even know I'm here."

The doctor said, "There is a phone in the hall. Call him!" My doctor stated I would be having a heart catherization the following morning. Well, the results showed that I had three blockages—possibly four—on the left side of my heart and I needed heart bypass surgery. My left main artery was ninety-five percent blocked & the other three were sixty percent blocked.

Surgery was scheduled for Wednesday morning. My pastor and his wife were with me and my husband when we were told what was going to be done. After the surgeon left we had prayer. During the prayer I felt peace within my soul and knew at that time that God was in control and I was not afraid anymore.

To make a long story short, I had my quadruple bypass surgery early Wednesday morning without any problems. By midnight I was standing, I moved out of the ICU early Thursday, and I got to go home on Sunday morning. My surgeon's assistant stated I was a walking time bomb.

I know that if my guardian angel (my boss) had not insisted I go to the doctor, I might not be here now. If God had not been with me, my husband, and the doctors, things would not have turned out this great.

I have been so blessed to still be working. I have been doing great ever since I had my heart bypass surgery on March 2, 2004, at the age of fifty-one. God is so good!

We give all the praise and glory to God! All we have to do is pray to our Lord and Savior every minute of the day and He will always take care of us.

Karen L. Williamson lives in Dry Prong, Louisiana, with her husband, James, to whom she has been married to for twenty-eight years. They have one son, Chad. The family attends Rock Hill Nondenomination Church in Colfax.

Ask God First

By Roger Wilson

When I was about twenty years old, I acquired a severe pain in my left shoulder. I could not throw or lift my arm straight out to the side. Reaching my arm out the window of the car at a drive thru was very painful.

I went to several doctors, and they did every test they could and found nothing wrong. So I went the next twenty-two years just living with the pain. Then, one day as I got out of bed, I found I could not lift my arm without there being sharp pain. I went back to my doctor, and he was unable to help me. Then I came to my senses and cried out to God for healing.

The next morning when I awoke, the pain was gone. Praise the Lord! I am now fifty-two. I can move my arm and shoulder in any direction and there is no pain. Doctors are wonderful and God uses them, but give God the first shot to get the glory.

Roger Wilson resides in Tremont, Mississippi, and is self-employed. He enjoys gardening and the country living.

Prodigal Daughter

By Jo Etta Woodall

It was December 1, 2002. My phone rang. It was my one and only child, my daughter. The conversation started out with "Mother, I don't want to have anything else to do with you. I don't want you to call me or see me." Also, I could no longer see my four-year-old grandson who I had been watching for her for four years.

She began to tell me how awful I was. You have to understand—my daughter and I were very close. I don't have words to describe to you how I felt. I can tell you it felt like someone had just cut my heart totally out. I had never experienced pain like that.

My daughter was married. Her husband was very controlling. I immediately cried out to God. I truly cried, "Oh Father, help me." Neither my husband nor I one could understand what could have gone wrong. I had my church, family, and friends all praying. We were pleading with God for help.

Every day and most nights I spent in prayer. I kept feeling as God was saying, "Wait." That came through so loudly to me: "Wait."

Finally, on April 7, 2004, I received a phone call from my daughter saying she wanted to see me. Like the prodigal father in Luke 15, I shouted for glory. It turned out my daughter's husband of fourteen years was an abuser. We didn't have a clue.

On April 7, 2004, my prodigal daughter returned. I am still giving God praise and glory. There is no a doubt in my mind God protected her and her son. God brought them back to us. All I can say is glory to God in the highest.

Jo Etta Woodall lives in Sherman, Texas. She is a born again Christian.

God Is Faithful

By Anonymous

Looking back over the past nine years, I can see how God's been faithful and is always there to see us through.

I married "in the church" and would have never dreamed what was ahead, but God knew and had a plan in mind despite my impending heartache and pain.

Nearly fifteen years into my marriage, I was left with four sons to raise—ages three to thirteen—so that my husband might pursue what some call an "alternate lifestyle." It was heartbreaking, but God gave me sustaining grace through many trials. He even put a cross in the sky in the form of a cloud on what would have been our anniversary. It told me this, "It is I the Lord God who goes before thee. I will not forsake you."

God took care of court issues related to support, custody, and more. I knew He was on my side and that He looked after His own. I prayed "power of the blood protection" on my sons before they visited their dad and saw it work many times. God has seen me through teen rebellion and a prodigal son who has since returned to our lives. He has also given me a real ministry as a result.

Shortly after my husband left, God, according to Ps. 40:3 and II Cor. 1:3-4, inspired me to write many new songs. He allowed me to meet folks who could sing and record them in order to further bless many more people. What an opportunity! Something good can come from pain.

God is good! We could dwell on problems, but that would not fix things, or we can look to God for strength to go on.

Are we pliable clay in the Potter's hand? When trials come, do we let them shape us, knowing He sees the final product? Do we trust

Him? Are we willing to be used for His glory, and not our own? He has a glorious plan and will work with pliable clay (our trials) if we let Him. Will we be useful, willing vessels?

Life is never easy. There are still trials even now, but I look forward to the promise of heaven some day. I still pray for my sons and their father that they receive grace, God's will, and more. I'm thankful for the ministry of song and look forward to what He will do.

The author is a single mother with four sons. She lives in Thomasville, Pennsylvania.

Printed in the United States
88160LV00005B/16-78/A